THE LOGICAL JOURNEY TO
HAPPINESS

THE LOGICAL JOURNEY TO
HAPPINESS

A Question Book

SHANE DILLON

LOGICAL
JOURNEY
PUBLISHING

FORWARD

In "The Logical Journey", each person is the keeper of their own happiness. With every choice, we give ourselves permission to decrease or eliminate the things that do not bring happiness into our lives. Each of us chooses happiness, or not, with every decision we make. It would be easy to think we could blame our unhappiness on someone else (our spouse, parents, boss, or children). If that were the case, no individual would ever be responsible for their own happiness. There would be no logical journey to happiness. We would be stuck, unable to make the changes in our lives that could lead us to happiness. "The Logical Journey" makes it clear. We can choose to start on our path to happiness today.

As time is our most valuable asset, we can choose to do more of the things we love. Even if we can't eliminate everything that does bring unhappiness into our lives, we can develop our own step-by-step plan that will put us on the path. Each of us chooses the rate at which we approach the planning process. This is why it is important to be ready to write as soon as you start reading the questions. Keep your "Logical Journey" with you always to reflect your thought processes as they evolve.

It is true: life is about the people you meet, the love you share, the books you read, the places you travel, the things you create, the art you enjoy. These are the choices we make each day to enrich our lives.

The book is written in question format, which leads the reader on their own journey to find the answers to questions they may have asked themselves in the past but were not prepared to answer. Suggestions or recommendations are provided with some, but not all of the questions. It would be to the reader's advantage to have a journal or notebook on the ready when starting the book. The answers to the questions are within each of us. Some of the questions may be immediately pertinent to the reader, while other questions may remain unanswered until the reader is ready. Almost anyone can associate with the questions. Some are playful, light and humorous, while others may be of a very serious nature and may require some deep searching. Essentially, by answering the questions, the reader is taking their own personal journey to happiness and writing their own version of the book.

The author is writing from a positive perspective, yet discusses real-life, real-time issues that have been proven over time to affect a person's ability to achieve happiness based on the choices they make. The relevance of the questions may not be revealed to each reader at first. By looking through the book, many references are made that could lead the reader to Aha! moments throughout. The book is a path to self-discovery. Through the reader's own logical journey, they can share happiness with the other inhabitants of the universe and find peace, improve health, and enhance mindfulness.

On a more personal note, about one month into editing "The Logical Journey" I was diagnosed with breast cancer. I immediately recognized the opportunity to edit this uplifting book was a gift. The questions and the writing spoke to me. How can a person be happy after being diagnosed with breast cancer? Going through my editing process, I found that almost every question was relatable. I found myself picking up a pen, opening my journal, and finding solutions to my new problems. Before long, I was expounding on the simple wisdom of the questions. Maybe I can go through this breast cancer trauma and be unafraid, even happy! Maybe I can find a way to let spirituality back into my life. Maybe someone could find a solution for loneliness and find happiness. Maybe a person could rid themselves of guilt (important for women, but men carry a lot of guilt, too!). Maybe we can help each other and, therefore, help ourselves find happiness. Maybe just one person can make changes that affect others and change the world!

We are all on a personal journey to happiness. For me, the most important discovery on the path to happiness is through the choices I make every hour, every day, every year. I have become more conscious of choosing happiness whenever possible.

Are you ready to start your logical journey to happiness?

Forward by:
MICHELE R. GIDCUMB
Creative Editor

THE LOGICAL JOURNEY TO
HAPPINESS

A Question Book

TO BEGIN IS TO CHANGE

1

Are you ready? How do you define happiness? Do you have the ability to create happiness in your current situation? Are you willing to take small steps to reach big goals over time? Did you know you can achieve happiness through the choices you make every day? Every week? Every year? Do you spend too much money on stuff that ends up buried in a closet or cabinet? Do you wish you had saved your money instead of going into debt for that fancy car or expensive house? Are you kind? Are you willing to help others in need? Do you wish you could afford to travel to the places you have always longed to see? Did you know that each of us is responsible for our own happiness, and has the ability to make changes in our lives that lead us on a logical path to happiness?

2

Would you agree that 10% of happiness is external and 90% is internal? Do you think you can be happy externally if you are not internally happy? Where does internal happiness come from?

People need to have a purpose in life. When we find our purpose and pursue it with a passion we are almost always happy. Don't wait for happiness to come to you. Find your purpose and go get it!

3

Do you think you are average? Are you happy being average? If no one thinks they are average, why is everyone so afraid to be different or to stand out?

The logic behind this question is maddening. We're all unique, yet hardly any of us ever takes a chance to express our uniqueness. It's easy to be average. You never have to take chances, just sit back and watch other people fail and succeed. Figure out your life's purpose or a life goal to work toward. There's nothing wrong with a little average in your life, just don't let it take over!

4

Have you ever thought about the idea that life is like a video game? In video games, we follow excitement. Isn't that what we do in life? Do you ever notice the repetitions in life?

At least 75% of your day is a routine. Think about it. If you sleep for 8 hours each day, that's 33% of your day. Then you go to work for 8 hours, but it takes you at least an hour before and after work to get ready and commute to work. You're up to 18 hours or 75% of your day! Get out of your routine and enjoy new things. You'll be a happier person for it. As for the other 25% of your day, make sure to maximize it by learning, chasing excitement, and bringing more happiness into your life.

5

What foods make you feel healthy or energized? What foods make you feel bad or tired?

Keep a list of each on your phone or in a notebook. Once you begin to see a pattern, then eliminate the bad foods from your diet and replace them with more of the healthy foods which make you feel better. Our bodies are complex machines that perform better when we fuel it with a healthy, balanced diet. If in the beginning, you don't like vegetables, it won't take long before you learn to love them and your body starts craving them. Our bodies know what foods it needs to run optimally, so listen to your body and give it what it needs.

6

Do you still believe you are insignificant?

It is theorized the human brain has as many neurons as there are stars in the Milky Way Galaxy. Also, your brain has as many synapses as the entire universe. What a powerful thought. You are more special than you ever imagined. Embrace life for how precious it is and experience it to the fullest. The world is a huge mystery and it is your playground. Go out and discover it!

7

Do alcohol, cigarettes, marijuana, and other drugs make you feel happy? What about coffee, does it make you feel happy? Or the internet? Or television?

It is amazing how many times we don't stop to think about the purpose of what we do. If time is your most valuable asset, why do you think we are always just trying to fill it up with something? We never really stop to think about the purpose behind that substance and if it brings happiness into our lives.

8

What made people happy a hundred years ago? Is it similar to what makes people happy today? In a hundred years in the future, what do you think will make people happy?

Perhaps what makes people happy will evolve, but one thing will remain the same. Only you can make yourself happy.

9

What are you the best at? Do you get enjoyment from being the best? Do you learn more by being bad at something, but just as passionate? Can you think of something you sucked at, but loved it anyway? Don't we suck at everything in the beginning?

Life is just one big lesson. If you don't like learning, then you probably aren't very happy. If you want to bring more happiness into your life, find something you are passionate about and learn everything you can about it.

10

Stop complaining and start a revolution! What is something exciting you can do today or this week? You have one life to live.

As you get older, more and more of your friends start to pass away. Stop waiting around for the world to offer you something. You've got to treat the world like an all you can eat buffet and take what you want. Follow excitement. Sign up for lessons or take a class. You've got to do it! Do something you have always wanted to do.

Be careful out there campers!

11

Have you ever thought of your life like a movie and you are the main character? What would your character portray? Would the movie be a comedy, sci-fi, action, or a drama? Are you the good guy or the bad guy? Would you be a rich guy or a superhero? Can you think of a time where you manifested something in your life?

Your life is created through your actions and thoughts. The power of manifestation is a powerful tool, don't be afraid of it. Remember: you write your own script.

12

Can you remember the last time you woke up extremely early to catch a flight to go on vacation? Why do you think it is so easy to wake up early for a vacation but not for work? Why can't we capture the vacation feeling every day? How many times do you typically hit your snooze button in the morning? Are you going to bed on time?

Sleep plays a major role in your happiness. Try to be conscious of how much sleep you are getting and how to improve the quality of your sleep. Alcohol is horrible for sleep. Exercise is good for sleep.

13

What is the happiest memory you have with your mom when you were a kid? Your dad? Your brothers? Your sisters? Your pets? Do you think you remember the happiest or the most tragic memories? How do your memories shape your decision making in life?

Our memories are very selective. It is interesting that we forget 90% of what we learn and do.

14

How does a millionaire wash their hands? How do you wash your hands?

There are 7.5 billion people on this planet. Money doesn't make a person better or worse. The key to a happy and fulfilling life lies within each of us. We don't have the power to change the past, but we do have the power to change the future. Ensure you are consciously finding ways to improve your spirit and positivity to the world.

15

How many hours of television do you watch on average per day? How much happiness does watching television bring into your life? Or is it just a way to take your mind off of what is important? Do you think you could be an expert at something else if you spent those hours learning or practicing something you are passionate about?

The average American watches 4 hours of television per day, which is 28 hours a week or 1,460 hours per year. You could learn to play the guitar, paint, write books, or become a better investor. It is easy to complain about not having enough time in life, but the reality of the matter is you control your life and the time in it. Look at your life and make sure there is a purpose in the activities you choose to spend time on, with happiness being the main purpose.

16

Would it make you happy to write in a morning journal?

If you haven't tried it, pick up a notebook and do it for one week. Wake up fifteen minutes earlier than usual and start writing on one of the topics discussed in this book. Writing is a powerful form of meditation which makes you think in the present moment and provides you an opportunity to reflect and analyze events and emotions in your life. Writing also aids your organizational skills. By writing in the morning, you are starting the day with a clear head and you know what your purpose for the day will be.

17

What physical possessions do you really need in order to be happy? Are you a slave to money?

When we take out student loans, car loans, and mortgages, we are not only borrowing money but sacrificing hours of our lives in the form of work. The banks are getting rich from your debts. They are charging you interest and reinvesting it into other financial vehicles. The more money the banks lend, the richer they become.

18

When was the last time you enjoyed a long kiss or hug? Why do you think the need for physical affection is hardwired in each of us?

Research has shown that hugging relieves stress and lowers blood pressure. The human body is the result of 4.5 billion years of evolution. We are amazing creatures programmed to adapt to many different situations and environments. Don't go against billions of years of evolution. Make sure you are using such tools as hugging and kissing to make yourself and others feel better.

19

What if wealth wasn't a physical or monetary thing, but rather something based on a happiness currency? Would you be rich or poor? Would you treat others differently? How would you pay for groceries? The more happiness you give, the more you will receive. How does that train of thought apply to your life today?

20

What is the farthest distance you have walked, ran, or cycled? Was it for enjoyment or out of necessity? Have you ever wanted to ride your bike across your state or country? Does a long journey sound like fun to you or hard work? Would you rather spend your money on a weekend romp to Berlin or take a month to cycle along the Danube in Germany?

Slow travel is the concept of fully immersing yourself in the travel experience to maximize and prolong the depth of the experience. Slow travel must be expensive. Wrong, the slower you travel the cheaper it is, walking being the cheapest and cycling being a close second. We're all different. The most important part of traveling is to continue to learn and to explore!

21

Have you ever read *Self-Reliance* by Ralph Waldo Emerson?

In *Self-Reliance*, Emerson urges his readers to be individuals and to think for themselves, and not to live to meet the expectations of others. The essay highlights the importance of following one's own voice, instinct, and ideas while working on developing your own individual character. Emerson also covers the downfall of debt and how it can rob one of self-confidence and the opportunity to succeed in life. *Self-Reliance* was written in 1841 but is more relevant today than ever.

22

Why don't we smile all of the time?

Physically smiling changes your mood and the mood of those around you. Smiling attracts happiness. The simple act of saying hello to others is proven to make you happier. Another way to bring more happiness in your life is by making a point to compliment your friends and family members. Maybe you can think of other simple acts that can bring more happiness into your life and those you encounter. Let's make the universe a little happier.

23

When was the last time you were conscious enough to feel and hear your heartbeat? Are you constantly living in the outside world or are you the type of person who likes to travel inward every once in a while?

Think about it, your heartbeat is always there but you rarely go inside to find it.

24

Are you a glass half-empty or a glass half-full person? Why does it matter?

We can't change the past, but we can change the present and the future. There is no value in regret. Fill'er up with happiness!

25

What are the things you most enjoy? What makes you happy? Do you do them in the morning or at night? What role does music and food play in your daily happiness? How many routines can you name off the top of your head?

Make it up as you go along. Don't overthink life. Follow excitement and do the things you most enjoy. If your life is one big routine, make sure it consists of happiness and not negativity.

Routines: sleep, food, commute, brush teeth, set alarm clock, do dishes, exercise, take a siesta, talk on the phone, etc…

Just about everything in your life is a routine, your life has a rhythm to it. Be conscious of your rhythm and optimize it to make you happy! All right, go!

26

When was the Wild West? When was Mozart alive? When was the Civil War? Who built the pyramids? What are you thinking about today? Who or what will our civilization be remembered for? What is the purpose of your life? Do you have a life project?

Too often we get caught up in our daily routines to ask the right questions. Make sure your daily routines are leading somewhere and not just in circles.

27

Do you feel like you are a bad public speaker?

Go online and take public speaking classes and start recording your speeches. The more you hear your voice on a recording, the more comfortable you will become with public speaking. Here's another idea, start recording a daily podcast for your ears only. It only takes five minutes out of your day and it is a great way to grow comfortable speaking your mind. We all have important things to say, it's just a matter of feeling comfortable speaking to your listeners.

28

Has there been a time in your life when you went from being the best at something to discovering that you were just a normal person? When and how did it play out? Does it make you happy to be recognized for your talents or do you prefer to fly under the radar?

The best high school basketball player in the state of Indiana went from being the best as a high schooler to average in college. The smartest kid in your high school graduating class goes from being number one to the bottom ninety-nine percent in college. There is always someone better, more proficient. Life is a frame of mind and our perceptions are easily distorted.

29

How much enjoyment do you get out of your cell phone? What apps or websites bring you the most joy? Do you feel productive or unproductive when you use your cell phone? Do you use it too much when you are bored? Are you more or less social because of your cell phone?

Take time to reflect on these questions. Pay attention to your answers and make a change based upon what makes you happiest.

30

Who is the one person in your life you are constantly seeking approval from? Is it necessary? How long have you known the person and does that person even know what makes you happy? Do you really care what other people think of you?

You only have to answer for what is right in your own head. Unconsciously, most people allow their confidence to be overrun by how they think other people perceive them. Most likely, the person perceives you completely different than you think. Plus, in the end, the other person is probably playing the same game in their head.

Confused yet? The point is that confidence should be produced from within and not based on the opinions of others. The best part, confidence is something you can practice and grow!

31

What is the oldest city you have ever traveled to? Did it feel like you were traveling back in time?

Damascus, Syria has been inhabited for over 11,000 years. The oldest city in the United States is St. Augustine, Florida, which was founded in 1565. As individuals, we have a hard time grasping time and place unless we have traveled to many other countries. It's been calculated there have been over 105 billion human births on earth since the beginning of time. A lot of people have lived before you and a lot of people will live after you. Make sure you are living your life to the fullest and that you are happy doing what you are doing!

32

What is your morning routine? Does your morning preparation put you in a positive frame of mind or do you just stumble out the door in a rush?

Here's what a healthy morning routine might look like.
  » Fifteen minutes of meditation
  » Fifteen minutes of stretching and pushups
  » Write one page in a morning journal

A morning routine brings clarity to your life and keeps you on track to achieve your goals. It is possibly the most important 45 minutes of your day. Make sure you have a journal and develop a morning routine that works for you. We're all different!

33

Get up and dance! Take the stairs! Walk to work! Ride your bike to the supermarket!

Use it or lose it. If you don't use your body, then it will slowly deteriorate and cause you pain. There is no excuse for laziness. It is never too late to make a change. If you are having problems with your weight, then slowly make changes in your life to improve your health. Find enjoyment in being mobile and free. The harder your body works, the more energy you will have in reserve.

34

When was the last time you slept underneath the stars? How old were you? Were you nervous? Where were you? Why are so many people afraid of sleeping in nature?

Not long ago, when people traveled long distances, they slept under the stars. Over time, people spend more and more time indoors. We like it to be 70 degrees all the time. Try sleeping under the stars for just one night. Maybe you will understand the value.

35

How do you pursue your personal goals? Have you designed a daily routine to help you achieve your goals? Do you have a short-term and a long-term plan for each one of these areas in your life?

Health, income, travel, social life, creativity, and education are a few areas in our lives that can lead us to happiness. Write them down and develop a system of tracking your goals. You will experience more in life and be a happier person for it!

For example, when it comes to health your goal might be to run a marathon or simply just exercise for thirty minutes each day. Your income goal might be to save enough to become financially independent or to save thirty percent of your paycheck each week. Write them down and come up with a system to track your goals. Make it a routine by writing in a morning journal or start your own personal podcast for your ears only! Give it a go!

36

Who was the best teacher you ever had in school? What do you think made them a good teacher? Were you able to relax and have fun? Do you think being fun is a good quality to have as a teacher? In your life, do you teach, whether it is to kids or coworkers? What is your teaching style?

Make sure you are having fun and you will leave a lasting impression.

37

Have you ever noticed how happy children are? What makes their happiness so pure? Do you think we can learn from children? Wouldn't it be interesting to see a chart mapping "happiness" from birth to death? How do you think your chart would look?

Children are generally happy by nature. Perhaps adults are wise. Both can benefit from each other. Include children in your life. Maybe you could improve your happiness quotient!

38

Do you have self-remedies to make yourself happy? What are they?

Going for a long walk is a good way to relieve stress. Others use meditation to center themselves. Keeping a gratitude journal is another way to remind yourself of the things for which you are grateful. Exercise and the arts are powerful self-remedies. Television and alcohol—not so much. Make sure you are doing things which make you feel happy and healthy. Following the media and the masses, medicating with legal and illegal drugs can quickly become an anti-happiness habit. Choose your self-remedies wisely!

39

When is the last time you walked barefooted along the beach or in nature? Did it make you happy? Did you feel more connected to the earth, the wind, the weather, and your surroundings?

You don't have to go very far to find happiness, just step outside to nature.

40

Can you think of a time you got into an argument with a friend that ended with both of you being upset?

In the right circumstances, critical feedback may lead to self-improvement. It may help us to do better. We overreact when the criticism points to one of our wounds, it is a defense mechanism. Learn to be non-reactive in the face of criticism and to use it to improve your life. You will be happier for it! You have more to learn by approaching a debate with an open mind than foolishly arguing with a friend.

41

If you donated or threw out one thing each day that you didn't need or use, how many days in a row could you throw something out?

Minimalism can actually be very liberating!

42

Can you think of someone who may have been the happiest person in history? Why? Was it because that person owned a lot of material possessions? Was that person rich?

Happiness is a skill to be learned. Practice and you will get better. Define what makes you happy. Mold your mind and train it to be happy. Next time you are happy, write it down. Maybe keep a little pocket journal to write down all of your happy moments. Once you have a list of happy moments, start practicing them over and over. You will be surprised how good you can get at being happy!

43

How many things in your life do not bring you happiness? Make a list.

For example: lack of money, being sick or unhealthy, feeling overweight, loss of rights, personal suffering or the suffering of others.

Now that you have made your list, write the opposite of each beside each item on your list. Find ways to move from the negative side of your list to the positive. Remember, energy is neither created nor destroyed. Whether you choose to use energy in positive or negative ways is up to you.

44

What role does love play in happiness? Why do you think there are so many songs and stories written about love? Is love the closest we get to happiness? Why do you think love is an emotion hardwired in the human brain?

Love is one of the keys to evolution. For human beings, love is biological, we have the need to protect and nurture those we love for the purpose of procreation. Love is the root cause of "survival of the fittest". The more love you to bring the world, the more you will receive. Find people in your life to love and keep them close. Don't be afraid to love.

45

Can you think of something that happened last week that upset you? Does it matter today?

Think about the situation that made you the most pissed off for the whole year. You probably can't remember. It's funny how a little time heals almost everything. Maybe it isn't that "time" heals all. It's just that the love in us is overtaking the hatred. Love is a powerful thing. I don't think we can fully grasp the purpose of love in our lives.

Next time you are mad, just stop and think about how you will feel tomorrow or next week. Is it still worth it?

46

Do you remember the feeling when you first learned to ride a bike or swim? Can you think back to what your first bike looked like? How about getting your driver's license? What milestones are you working toward in your life today?

Certain milestones in life are unforgettable. List two to three life-changing projects you have in the pipeline right now. Learn new things continuously. It's exciting and you are a better person for it!

47

If you could live anywhere in the world, where would it be? Why? What would you do for fun? How does that differ from where you live now? What factors go into living in a good place? Do you take the cost of living into consideration when it comes to the city or town you live in? How far have you moved from your hometown? Do you think people who live close to their childhood home are happier than people who move away? What is the one thing in the world that you cannot live without? Is it a physical possession or maybe a person? How does this thing or person contribute to your daily happiness?

The average American never moves farther than twenty miles from their hometown. A lot of things in life are taken for granted. Make sure you are showing your appreciation for the things you have and the people you love.

48

Have you ever tried being a vegetarian or a vegan?

Try it for a day or a week, for no other reason than to experience life. Your body is a complex organism which needs healthy food. Eating meat and potatoes will not cut it. Along with a healthy diet, make sure you are at least breaking one sweat a day. Your body is your vehicle for the rest of your life. You can't live without it and it can't go on without your consciousness. A healthy diet and exercising contribute to your happiness level.

49

Describe your childhood house? What is the best memory you have of it? Did you share a bedroom with a sibling? Were there a lot of neighborhood kids around? What games did you play in the hood?

As kids, we have more free time and more opportunities to develop friendships. Life doesn't have to be that way. As an adult, fight to bring more free time into your life and to be a friend. Remember…let's keep laughing, let's keep smiling, let's keep loving!

50

Do you enjoy waking up every morning?

Get up and wake up and live! Don't complicate your thoughts, we're here to live and experience. We should all be excited to wake up every morning to see what the day brings. Life is a gift. It is sad to think we waste a third of our lives sleeping. By learning ways to maximize your happiness, you'll find yourself waking up earlier and earlier each day. If you are the type of person who has a hard time waking up in the morning, try going to sleep earlier or wake up and do some jumping jacks. A lot of times by lying in bed longer you are altering your mood for the day. Stop! Get up and live! You were given this gift to live, love, and be happy.

51

What is stopping you? Have you ever wanted to do an extreme journey like the Pacific Crest Trail or a cross country bicycle ride? Is it physical, financial, mental, emotional, or that you just don't have time?

If it is physical, you might be relieved to learn about the Danube Bike Route in Germany; it is a paved bike path with very little elevation change. If your excuse is time, then only you can make the changes needed to make it happen. Bicycle touring and hiking are the cheapest forms of travel and quite possibly the most beneficial. Find time, you will never regret it!

52

Can you remember a Halloween when you dressed up in a costume and felt like a different person?

Maybe it was the mask or maybe it was having your face painted. In a matter of minutes, you were transformed into someone else. Each of us has the power to make a change in life, it just takes shifting your perception and looking at things a little differently. Your ability to change is greater than you would ever imagine. If you are not happy with your current circumstances in life, make a change. Don't sit around waiting for someone else to make the change for you because that will never happen. Be a doer and not doubter.

53

Could you be happy living in another country? Why do so few people have a passport?

So many people spend their lives repeating the same actions day after day, whether at work or at home. Create new chapters in your life. Go live abroad. Learn a second language. Become an explorer or a tour guide. Volunteer on an organic farm in Hawaii. The world is your playground. Don't be afraid of the unknown!

54

Does getting accepted to a top tier university lead to happiness? How valuable is that degree from an elite university? Is it worth working twenty years to pay off your student loans? If seventy-percent of Americans are living paycheck-to-paycheck, do you think the college system is providing a good service to society?

55

Picture yourself as a wizard with unlimited powers. How would you use your powers to bring happiness into the world? What would be the first potion you would make? Why? Who or what does the potion benefit?

As conscious beings, we are capable of so much more. Use your gift as a wizard to improve the lives of others. Start by passing out smiles and compliments and watch the world transform in front of you.

56

How many days out of the year do you think you are truly happy? What if we came up with a happiness index where you monitored your daily happiness high's and low's each day? Do you think you would learn anything new about yourself?

Being conscious of our time and how we spend it is frequently overlooked. If you are always complaining about not enough time, start paying attention to how you are spending it. You will quickly figure out where all of your time is going and how many hours each that you are truly happy. Don't forget, you can be truly happy in your job, cleaning up the kitchen, or just reading a book, too.

57

How do you currently incorporate music into your life? Where and when do you listen to music?

It's amazing how certain songs infuse you with electric energy from the first word. Music is a powerful tool to guide your mood and energy. Experiment with listening to different types of music when you first wake up, don't stick to your same old playlist. Why not start by downloading a playlist of the top 100 songs of all time or a playlist of classical music. Expand your mind by expanding your playlist.

58

Do onions make your eyes water? Does asparagus make your urine stink? Does the thought of lemons make your mouth water?

We are simply animals; don't you ever forget it. What can you learn about happiness by observing other animals? What makes your dog or cat happy? There are a lot of things in life we have no control over, yet we try to control everything. In the end, we're just another animal walking the earth in search of food, shelter, love, and happiness. Here are a few things: affection, food, exercise, work, spirituality, and social interaction. Why don't you start building your own happiness by addressing these simple activities?

59

What journey are you currently on?

There's work to be done. Life's work gets done little by little. The pyramids weren't built in a day. So don't get frustrated. If you can't bend life to your liking in a day or a week, keep up the good work! The fun is in the journey, not the destination.

60

Does fear prohibit happiness? What are you most fearful of? Do you fear rejection, uncertainty, being judged, failing, change, something bad happening, getting hurt? How can you eliminate your fears?

Would you be happier? Do you think you could live without television? How do you even benefit from having a television? Think about it: is there a link between fear and laziness? Are lazier people more apt to live in fear? Is television the source of our fears or a distraction from problem-solving?

Watching the news on television promotes fear and negativity. Try talking it out or write it in a morning journal to find the answer. Unfortunately, reflection is a tool rarely used. The tool most people use is television or alcohol as their therapist. Learn to become an independent thinker and develop a lifestyle of happiness.

"Fear is the path to the dark side. Fear leads to anger. Anger leads to hate. Hate leads to suffering." –Yoda

61

What are the happiest 10% of the people in the world doing differently than 90% of us who struggle to find happiness? How can you join the happiest 10% of the people in the world?

Set goals, exercise daily, surround yourself with positive influences, don't be afraid of change, seek a coach or mentor, learn new things, be brave, follow excitement, actively pursue happiness! Model your life after the happiest 10% and you will soon have the life of the happiest 10%.

Idea: Carry a card in your pocket with a list of things that contribute to your happiness. Look at your happy card often and add to it anytime you find a new piece of happiness. Your goal should be to fill up your happiness card and have to start carrying multiple cards in your pocket!

Happiness is a choice you must make every hour, every week, every year, for the rest of your life.

62

How many things in your closet have you not worn in the last year? In the last five years? Why do we feel the need to collect unnecessary stuff? Are your cabinets so stuffed that when you open them things fall out onto your head?

More stuff doesn't make us happier. If anything it is a reminder of wasted time and money. Be thoughtful and make smart buying decisions. Only buy the things you truly need that is well made and useful.

63

How long do you want to work? Do you love what you do for a living? What does your dream job look like? How many hours would you work? What would be your title?

Do not settle for a job because it pays the bills. If you have no other options, then continually work to improve and prepare for advancement. More or less, you use the same amount of energy each day. Maximize your energy potential. Spend time visualizing your goals and start working toward achieving them! Save whatever you can manage by not buying more stuff you probably don't need. Plan how you can retire early from savings and investments. Others do it every day. So can you!

64

If you could meet any three people from any time in history, who would they be? Why would you like to meet them? Do they possess any qualities you can bring into your life? Do you attract friends with similar attributes?

Surround yourself with people who compliment you and make your life complete. Find people with whom you can grow and discuss life's challenges. But never discount someone because they don't share your views. Some of the most precious times in life are conversations. Very often, a person with opposing views is a learning opportunity. A conversation is proof you don't necessarily need physical things to bring happiness into your life.

65

Have you been to India? France? Iceland? New Zealand? Do you want to go?

Experience life! You can take memories with you wherever you go compared with most physical possessions, which become dated or worn out. Make two lists, one list for life experiences you have done in the past, the second list for places and things you would like to do. Writing our dreams and visions down is a powerful tool which is not used often enough. Something about writing an idea down makes it happen. Another tool to make your travels become a reality is to start telling people your ideas. For example, if you want to bicycle across the United States, then start telling people you want to do it. The more we put our dreams out into the world, the more likely they are to become a reality. Only you can make your dreams come true!

66

What are your top five songs of all time? Who were the musicians that played them? What other bands did those musicians play in during their career?

Too often we just scratch the surface of the things we love. If you find a musician or an artist you like, learn all about them. Who knows, you might just find you have more in common with them than you ever thought. Creative people are thinkers who live in the present moment. You can learn a lot from their art, work and also from their lives. Be curious, keep learning, and follow the things that make you happy!

67

When was the last time that you watched live footage of Woodstock or another epic concert?

Take time to appreciate the past; believe it or not, they were driven by the same energy we are. That's right! Energy can neither be created nor destroyed. Energy has momentum. All energy originates from the sun. When you spend time watching the videos of live concerts like Woodstock, that energy is being transferred to you. I'm no expert, but this all sounds good to me!

68

Remember being a kid and making a fort out of blankets and pillows? As an adult, what have you replaced with those sorts of games?

Please don't say reality shows or sports on TV. If you are too tired to do anything during your free time, then you are doing yourself a disservice. We were not put on this planet to solely work. Time is a finite resource, make sure you are managing it to maximize happiness. If all you do is work, then what is your purpose? Time with family and friends is of much more value. Fight for your time! Live for your dreams!

69

What if criticism didn't exist in your life? Would you continue to improve? What purpose does criticism serve?

We learn from our own mistakes and it is important to know when we've made a mistake. Don't be too critical of yourself. Also, be conscious of where the criticism is coming from. If the criticism is coming from the wrong source it can cause more harm than good. Learning is made up of mistakes and improving on them. Criticism may push us to get better, just make sure you use it to fuel the fire, not put it out.

70

Can you dance to the beat? Do you remember when you first learned how to dance? Did it make you happy?

Are you, like me, the only person in a crowd of thousands that claps offbeat to the band! We have all been gifted a different set of skills—no one is perfect. The sooner you learn to accept who you are and the skills you were given, the stronger you will be. It's okay to suck at certain things. It's actually fun to suck at certain things. So why not embrace your suckiness when it brings happiness into your life! Dance like nobody's watching!

71

What was the single happiest minute of your life? Was it recently or a long time ago? Did you cry out of happiness? Who was there? Could you paint a picture of it?

Happiness is like people; it comes in different shapes and sizes. We all find happiness in different things. Some of us find happiness in helping others, while others find happiness in achieving an impossible goal. The important thing is to be able to identify what makes us happy and consciously work toward repeating and perfecting actions that lead us to happiness. Happiness is not a one-time thing! Happiness requires constant care and feeding!

72

Why are so many Americans dependent on debt?

Eighty percent of Americans die in debt. Yet, only thirty-three percent of Americans consider themselves happy! These statistics were pulled from a quick internet search and you can take what you want from them. The important thing is to be conscious of the variables in your life that contribute to your happiness or unhappiness. Owing debt may be one of the variables in your life that determines how happy you are. Be conscious!

73

What was your favorite subject in school? Is it still something you enjoy doing? Did you make a career out of it? What was your least favorite subject in school? Did it turn into a career? What do you think are the most important aspects to a successful career and life?

Public speaking and personal finance are two areas of study not taught nearly enough in grade school or high school but are arguably the most important skills in life. If you can get some training on your own through research, it will improve your chances for upgrading your skills.

74

Do you have a house plant or a tree in your yard that brings you happiness? It's amazing how slow they grow; we barely even notice them until they are twice as big. Does happiness grow the same way?

Happiness is like a plant. They both need sunlight and nutrients to grow. So, make sure you are taking care of your body and mental health.

75

How can you shift your mind in the direction you want it to go or a place that you want to be?

Everyone is against me. Stop thinking that. Something inside of you is stopping you from achieving your potential. Don't give in to those thoughts. Reading is a powerful tool to learn from others to produce more positivity and happiness in your life.

76

What is the prettiest rainbow you've ever seen? What gives a rainbow its various colors? Why is the sky blue? Where does the wind come from? What kind of tree is growing in the front yard? How many stars are in the galaxy? How do birds fly?

Be curious. Never stop asking questions. Become a lifetime learner.

77

If you could relive a day over and over, what day would it be? What was so special about that particular day? Who did you cross paths with during the day? What was the weather like? Where did you dine?

Maybe incorporate some of that day into your current day. By default, we will repeat the same day over and over countless times. That is what happens when you work the same job for forty years and live in the same house. You are bound to repeat your days. Make sure if you are repeating days over and over that they are the happy days!

78

Who is your favorite classical musician? You could start with Chopin, Liszt, and Bach.

If you are looking for a living musician in this genre, then check out Lang Lang, Ludovico Einaudi, and Yo-Yo Ma. These musicians are true rock stars, and it is a shame they are not recognized in the same light as rock and pop.

Here are some of the benefits of listening to classical music: Boosts creativity, improves memory, reduces stress, fights depression, increases productivity, makes you happy!

79

Have you ever gone on a vacation where there was no internet access? What was your initial reaction? Did you find it peaceful to be disconnected from the world? Did you think about things differently? What value does the internet provide outside of work? Are we better as a society for being connected all of the time? If not, then why are we all so addicted to our phones?

80

What muscles in your body ache? Do you think aching muscles are the result of stress or unhappiness? When you have an ache or a pain, how do you remedy it? After it has healed, are you proactive in exercising to prevent the ache from coming back? If our bodies act as a vehicle, then what is it transporting? Does that make our brain the onboard computer?

Our bodies are sophisticated machines that require not only repairs but upkeep and maintenance as well. Take care of your body! If our brains are a computer, then make sure you are continually reprogramming by learning. The more information and data points you can collect the better your computer will work. Learning equals happiness!

81

Can you identify your blockers to achieving true happiness?

Assumptions:

> » Each of us owns our happiness.
> » We cannot blame our happiness blockers on others (boss, mother, spouse, children).
> » Each of us is responsible for making the change in our lives that leads to increased happiness.

We create our own blockers. Maybe we are stubborn and won't admit we made a mistake. It could be easier to do nothing than to make an effort toward happiness. Perhaps we have never even considered that happiness is a choice that we have to choose every hour, every day, every year. Reflect on what your blockers to happiness are through meditation or journaling.

82

Are you happy with your current job? Do you feel like your job is allowing you to grow? Are you learning new things? Are you meeting new and interesting people? Is there the opportunity to provide input for making improvements? Do you like your boss? Do you feel well compensated for the work you do? Do you feel like your job allows you to provide a service or to help others? What is the purpose of the work you do? Are you satisfied after a day's work? Do you see yourself in this job in 5 years? 10 years? The rest of your life? Is there something you would rather be doing?

83

What are you working on? What happens if you fail? Fast forward a year. Now does that failure mean anything in your life?

Sometimes you have to rise above the present moment and see it for what it is. We all start with a vision in our minds with what we think a project should look like, but in reality it usually turns out much different. The more you practice the better you get. Work hard to get through the learning process to become an expert at something!

84

Did you speak to your mom or dad today? If that's not possible, did you speak to someone you love today?

Don't take the special people in your life for granted, because sometimes we don't realize how special people are until it is too late. If your grandparents and parents are still alive, make sure you ask them all the questions about their lives and experiences, then pass them onto your siblings and kids. Sadly, when a person dies so does most of their stories and knowledge. As the saying goes: "A person doesn't die until their name is spoken for the last time." If this is the case, make sure to speak of loved ones and make sure they live forever!

85

Do you have a vision board?

A vision board is deciding on a list of things you want to accomplish in your future life. It is a way to manifest your dreams in life. This is how you make one: Begin by writing down your dreams or sketching them out. Add photos or cut-outs from magazines. Next, paste them to a piece of poster board. Finally, hang it in a place where you will look at it every day. Over time, your visions become reality. Be careful what you ask for because your dreams just might come true. Don't believe me? Then try it!

86

When was the last time you went to the city library?

One of my favorite activities of all time is aimlessly meandering through the library and pulling random books off the shelves. Almost every book in the library was written by a different person who had something important to say. There are thousands of books, each one with a different perspective on the world. With technology in our face all of the time, it is easy to forget about libraries. Don't! A library is an amazing place, and the more time you spend in the library, the more you benefit.

87

Which do you get more happiness from: life or work? Or have you managed to combine your life into your life's work? How many vacation days do you get each year? Do you wish you had more vacation time?

For most people, you don't have to dislike your work and you don't have to work every week of the year. If you find yourself in this vicious cycle, then figure out ways to educate yourself to succeed at the job of your dreams. Don't listen to the haters. You don't have to suffer through a job you don't like. Get out there and find a way to happiness!

88

What was the most amazing sunset you ever experienced? Where were you and who were you with? Now, how about the most amazing sunrise? That's a little bit harder! Why do you think sunsets are so beautiful? Do you think it is because of the colors in the sky or that they are able to slow you down long enough to put you in the present moment?

Sunsets serve as everlasting memories in your lives. Think about it, there are very few things in life which imprint your mind like a sunset. Make sure you are finding time to enjoy the sunset with family, friends, and a good glass of wine. Embrace life!

89

Does drinking alcohol make you happier or does it just mask your unhappiness? Why do so many people depend on alcohol to be social? What does that say about our society if we are dependent on alcohol to talk to one another? What other things in our lives mask our happiness? For example, prescription drugs, video games, tv series, watching sports on TV, social media, etc...

Make conscious decisions. One can find enjoyment in alcohol and one can drown in it as well. Listen to what your body is telling you and you will be amazed how good it makes you feel!

90

What things in your life are you happy about today? What led to this happiness? Who were you with? How can you prolong that happiness to last longer the next time or make it happen more frequently?

Happiness can be a routine, just like any other activity in our day. Keep a small journal in your pocket to record your happy moments. Once you have a list of happy moments, develop a happiness schedule to follow. You will be amazed by how much happiness you can fit into a single day. Again, this practice goes back to being conscious and self-aware of the activities in your life.

91

Don't worry, you've got plenty of time…until you don't. Always for money, always for love. Don't forget about yourself. What is the last thing you did to make yourself happy? What is the last thing you did to make someone else happy? Can't remember? Well then, you'd better get to work!

92

Are you guilty? Did you do things you wish you hadn't done as a child? Do you blame yourself for how your kids turned out? Do you wish you would have made better grades in high school so you could have gone to college or a better college, and could have gotten a better job?

You know what? Pack up all that guilt in an old suitcase and give yourself permission to throw that suitcase into a very deep lake. Don't spend your life regretting things you can't change. Pat yourself on the back and be proud of your many successes.

93

Do you have a savings account? 401K? Investment portfolio? Would you rather live in the mountains or at the beach? Would you like to live in another country? Would you like to quit your job and retire early?

Do the math. Your choices are very limited if you are not managing your money and preparing for your financial future. Build your safety net. Start investing a percentage of your income every paycheck. You can choose the life you want to live! But first you have to make some really good financial decisions and develop a plan of your own.

94

Who is your favorite blogger or podcaster?

If you don't have one, you are missing out. Stop looking at the big news websites and seek out cool people who are writing about things of interest to you. When people write blogs or books, they are opening up and sharing their life experiences with you. That is part of the reason classic novels are everlasting. Blogs, podcasts, and classic books are like traveling through time and experiencing another place, other people all from the perspective of the writer.

95

Escape! Our lives are filled with ways to escape. What are some ways you can escape?

We use television to escape. Monday Night Football is an escape. The latest and greatest TV series is an escape. The internet is a tool more often used to forget about work rather than to do work. This type of escape is taking our minds off the things that are important to our personal development. We don't learn and therefore we don't grow.

Right now, write down three things you use to escape reality. Next, write down three things you could replace them with to bring more happiness into your life and make you a better person. Escape to something that is more productive!

96

Do you get enough sleep?

Sleep is one of the most important roads to happiness. Through sleep, your body re-charges, heals, dreams, re-wires, re-builds, repairs, rests, fights disease. Your brain needs sleep. Don't short-change your body by not getting enough sleep.

97

When was the last time you performed a random act of kindness? When was the last time someone did something kind for you? Did you feel better when you were the giver or the recipient?

Most likely, the feeling of helping someone in need gives a more powerful sense of pride and happiness. You don't have to look very far to find someone less fortunate than yourself and lend a helping hand. But it's also nice when someone is paying attention to your needs, too!

Some examples of random acts of kindness: being a courteous driver, helping someone carry groceries or packages, visiting the sick, teaching—of any kind.

98

Are you afraid? Do you wake up every night worrying? Are you terrified of making any change in your life? Are you concerned about what people think and live life according to how you think others would expect you to live? Do you want to make changes in your life, but have analysis paralysis and make excuses about taking risks?

Start small by taking risks that may not greatly affect your peace of mind. Try a weekend vacation to explore someplace relatively close by, but new and different. Maybe shop around for a job, just to see what is available. Many times what you are really afraid of is making a commitment. Repeat the mantra, "Change is good, change is inevitable."

99

Have you ever stayed up all night reading a book knowing that you had work or school the next day? What was it that kept you hooked? Have you gone back and read it again? Can you list a couple of authors that you would read again and again?

Very few authors have the gift to keep the reader's attention for hundreds of pages. Maybe Ken Follett, Isaac Asimov, or Kurt Vonnegut. Reading is so much better for you than watching TV. Why books are better: develops focus and concentration, builds your vocabulary, improves your imagination, increases your wisdom and ability to reason.

100

What is the first thing that comes to your mind when you read the words "time rich"? Do you feel time-rich or time-poor? Do you feel money-rich or money-poor? How do the two concepts relate? Are you conscious of your free time and how you use it? How does the way you spend your time contribute to your happiness?

Seventy-five percent of our days are tied up in sleep and work. Think about it! You sleep eight hours a day and work takes up another ten hours of your day, including the time you get ready and commute time. If you consider days out of the year, it comes to over 250 days. Time is your most valuable resource. If you are spending your free time watching TV or surfing the internet, you may want to make note of more valuable ways to spend your time.

101

How many times do you hit the snooze button in the morning? Do you think if you never hit the snooze button you could be happier? Can you remember a time in your life when you woke up every morning without an alarm clock? Were you happier during this period in your life? Why do depressed people sleep more? So many questions!

102

Do you make more or less sense as you get older? Do you become a better dancer as you get older? Do you become a better speaker as you get older? Do you feel more like an individual as you get older? What three things did you enjoy most about being a kid? Why not try to include them in your daily or weekly routines?

As we mature, we become more comfortable with who we are. Growing older is truly a gift or it can be a hindrance. All we can do is embrace aging and take full advantage of the time we have on this planet. Make sure to continue to include activities you enjoyed as a kid, as an adult. Frisbee, swimming, picnics, camping out.

There are even coloring books for adults now!

103

Do, you have healthcare insurance or another safety net to protect you and your family from a catastrophic event? What would it take for you to get this protection? What steps can you take today? Have you ever thought about how a catastrophic event could change your life forever and affect your journey to happiness?

104

Has war ever brought anyone happiness? Why do we insist on inflicting pain on other human beings? What are wars usually fought over? Money, power, religion, natural resources…are these things really worth dying for?

In war, both sides lose. Sometimes a generation of young, healthy men and women are killed. Human beings have consciousness. Each and every life is beyond precious. We should be coveting this gift we were given and working to make it last as long as possible. At some point, humans need to decide to work together and move forward in peace. War is not the answer.

105

What things in your life would you like to change or achieve but you feel are unattainable?

Maybe it just takes looking at the problem or task from a different angle. Try to break down mountainous tasks into simple, daily tasks. Make sure you are setting daily goals which are achievable and allow you to build confidence. You are capable of more than you can ever imagine! Just open the Guinness Book of World Records, it's full of normal people accomplishing amazing feats. Don't sit back and let your life pass you by. Make sure you are living life on your terms and filling your hours, days, years with happiness!

106

What is the most difficult thing you have ever done in your life? Is it a challenge you choose for yourself or caused by an unexpected tragedy? Have you ever faced death? Are you better or worse for it?

After facing extreme adversity, people tend to appreciate the smaller things in life more. You may know someone with an awareness of the meaning or purpose of life after being put to the test.

107

Did you do anything creative today or this week? What was it? Do you get happiness from being creative?

There are many ways to be creative. The obvious ways are painting, writing, photography, music, dance, etc… the not so obvious ways are making cupcakes, playing with the shapes in the clouds, installing guerilla art, building a fort with your kids, making your own Halloween costume, or acting like a pirate for a day! Kids are filled with creativity, but unfortunately, as adults, our imagination is pushed aside for work and responsibilities.

Never stop creating. The day you stop creating is the day you die!

108

Do you spend quality time worrying about things that are not within your control? What's the matter?

Stop resisting, surrender your fears and move on. You're wasting precious time letting your worries consume you. Picture negativity as a big water bubble approaching you. When it hits you, the bubble explodes and ceases to exist. You will be a happier person for it.

109

Do you have a garden? A houseplant? Do you live someplace where you can watch living plants grow?

Perhaps you can walk in a park during a break from work or on your way home. Taking care of plants or even watching them grow can bring a moment of peace in your otherwise hectic life. Plants can be meditative, and a reminder that life is precious.

110

Did you grow up playing sports or playing an instrument? How did that activity influence your life? Are you a better person for it? If you could go back in time, what one sport or instrument would you tell your younger self to pursue? Well, what are you waiting for?

You are never too old to learn and to create. Go out and pick up the instrument you have always wanted to play now! Dig out your old baseball glove and go play catch. Be a doer!

111

Have you ever thought about taking a year off of work? What do you think you would gain by taking a year off of work to travel the world? Do you think your life would change for the better or worse? Would you go back to your old job or do something new?

It's not as hard as you think. It just takes a little planning and a lot of determination! Life is full of adventures; you just have to seek them out.

112

Who is your favorite band? How does your favorite band make you feel when you listen to them?

Take time to listen to every album they have ever produced. It is an interesting way to see the evolution of their music and art. Then take the time to write or paint while listening to them. Art is an amazing form of happiness that leads to nuggets of creativity we can pass on to other like minds.

113

What is your best quality?

Most of us know what others like about us. Maybe it is the ability to bring people together as a group, or that you can summarize the best ideas into a way forward. You may be the most compassionate when someone you love needs help. Make note of your best qualities and share them frequently. Don't keep these qualities to yourself.

114

Did you take a gap year after high school? If not, do you regret it? If you did, how did it change your life?

A gap year is taking a year off from school or work to travel the world and to find yourself. Gap years are more commonly taken by students in Europe. Your life is not all about making money, so don't waste your valuable time working every year from graduation to retirement. Spend time traveling and exploring more frequently. You'll be better for it.

115

When was the last time you expressed gratitude to someone?

Show gratitude to those who bring happiness into your life. List five people you are grateful for and why. Then let them know!

116

How many physical possessions does a person actually need to be content? Could you be content if all your possessions fit in two bags? Why or why not? Remember how little you survived on as a college student? What do you need in life to be happy? Are they physical things, life experiences, people, or emotions?

It is a good experience to take a long journey with only one or two bags of possessions to figure out what you really need in life. Don't be afraid to strip down your life to the basics and to rebuild it from there.

117

How big are your problems? How can we help others?

When you are feeling depressed, make a conscious decision to help others in need and see how it makes you feel! There are people in the world without potable water and electricity. There's enough food on the planet to feed everyone, yet people are still starving. There are others who have been incarcerated for most of their lives. There are more homes than people on the planet, yet people are still homeless. Think of one small solution, one difference you can make each day.

118

Growing up, did you feel like other families were wealthier than yours? Had nicer clothes, parents had better vehicles, better homes? Do you still feel this way?

It's a very normal feeling for kids (adults, too!) to have. Unfortunately, some of us have a harder time than others getting over it. Having more and better stuff doesn't make you a better person. It's time to pay attention to your own personal happiness. Name the things that bring joy into your life. You will likely find that those things have nothing to do with the amount of stuff you own.

119

Do you have a favorite mantra?

A mantra is soothing words that give you comfort and peace and aids in meditation, prayer, or reflection. A mantra can be as simple as, "Love, peace, joy." Some may say that a mantra is a blessing you give to yourself. My favorite mantra is from a book by Jack Kornfield, entitled "A Path With Heart". It goes like this:

"May I be filled with loving-kindness. May I be safe from inner and outer dangers. May I be well, in body and mind. May I be at ease and happy."

Write these words down and carry them with you wherever you go. Better yet, commit these words to memory.

120

Have you ever taken the time to define what happiness means for you? What was your definition of happiness when you were five or sixteen versus today? What's different in your life?

The quest for happiness is coded into our DNA. It gives us something to work toward and a reason to continuously learn new things. Learning is happiness.

121

Have you ever taken a walking meditation?

Be aware of a park, woods, or creek near your residence that brings you peace. Schedule time to go there frequently and just be alive. Meditation is the art of not thinking and requires practice. Once you develop the skill of meditation, it becomes necessary for happiness.

122

Are you a morning or a night person? Why? What kind of stuff makes you a morning or a night person? When are you most creative and think most clearly? What makes one person more creative than another? How do our parents, childhoods, affect our creativity as adults?

Everyone is different and we are motivated by different things in our lives. Taking advantage of these natural tendencies should be a priority. For example, if you do your best work at night, plan more free time or "me time" when you can be most productive.

123

Have you ever stayed up all night working on a project? What was it?

Studying for a test doesn't count! I'm talking about a time you were so excited to stay up all night on your own terms. Or, maybe you stayed up all night trying to finish a book! It's amazing how some things can tap an unknown energy source in your body. Music does this, too. This may be a good place to start thinking about what brings joy to your life.

124

Can you recall a time when you were stuck in extreme weather? What did you do? Who were you with? Looking back on it, how did you make the most out of a bad situation? Why do you think that is? Is it a defense mechanism to teach us lessons from the past?

The extreme moments in our lives tend to stick out in our memories, like the camping trip from hell. Maybe such experiences are most memorable because you learned self-reliance or figured out how to rise above the worst that could happen. Life is filled with opportunities to learn.

125

What is the purest form of happiness you have experienced? How would you define happiness?

Write down five things that made you happy today or this week. Now, is there a way that you can relive or prolong your pure happiness every day?

126

Do you do what makes you happy or what people expect of you?

You are the CEO (Chief Executive Officer) of your own happiness. You make the decisions and live with the consequences. No one is your boss when it comes to your happiness.

127

What daily routines make you happy? What can you do to make your daily schedule more fun or interesting?

Here are a few suggestions: listening to upbeat music in the morning or singing in the shower, listening to a podcast, talking to your kids before you drop them off for school, biking to work instead of driving, planning a special meal for your family. Make sure your routines are filled with happy and meaningful activities.

128

Are you worthy? Do you deserve to be happy? Do you know what it will take to make you happy? Are you willing to make the choices that lead to your own happiness today, next week, next year?

129

When was the last time you organized an evening of entertainment for friends? Do you share mutual interests with friends or acquaintances?

Create a meal or appetizers with friends. Try making sushi with friends. Share a bottle of wine. Make sure you continue to grow and flourish along this journey of life. You're not alone. Stop living in fear and become a doer. Music, books, film—all important topics of conversation.

130

When was the last time you told a lie? Would you tell it again or was it a worthless lie to make you look or feel better? Can you think of someone you know who is constantly lying to others? How do you think they perceive themselves?

A lie is usually told when a person is uncomfortable with who they are and want others to think of them differently than they perceive themselves. A white lie here and there may not be the end of the world. Make sure you are not filling your life with one lie after another. Be conscious of your feelings toward yourself and address your insecurities when they are brought to your attention.

131

What are you waiting for? What's your plan for making changes in your life?

Stop waiting and approach your "passion" from as many different angles as you can possibly think of. Our lives are a series of chapters. Before you know it, one chapter ends and the next one begins. If we keep putting our passions on hold, before we know it the story moves on from us. Stop waiting and live a life full of purpose and learning.

132

How much happiness do you receive from the purchase of a new car, a big house, or clothes? Would you make the same purchase again or do you want your money back after a bit of time? What physical possession has brought you the most happiness? When you were a kid, did you have a bike or a skateboard that brought you a lot of happiness? Did you maintain your childhood bike, or did you ride it until you had a flat or something else broke on it?

Our physical possessions are extensions of our lives and it is interesting to figure out where our happiness is coming from. Once you target your happiness, then work on prolonging it or bring more of it into your life!

133

Did you know that you can change the world? Or, does the world cause you to change? Who's in control of all this? Can you think of a time when you envisioned something you wanted, and it came true? Where are you in your career path and where do you think it is going? What do you want your title to be? How much money would you like to make? Don't think it has to be chaos or that you are not in control.

You control more than you think! You are the person making the choices. Write down what you want your job to look like in one year. In five years.

134

What was the most miserable time of your life? What did you do to break free from this misery? Was it a person, a hobby, time, or money that broke you free from that depression?

Everyone has difficult times in life. It is in these times that we need to make sure to have a diversified happiness portfolio. Don't think of happiness as a single feeling coming from a single source. Happiness is all around you. Find happiness in as many things as possible. That way, if one stream of happiness breaks down, hopefully you have another stream you can draw from to help minimize the loss. Take a minute to define how many happiness streams are available to you.

135

When was the last time you were forgiven? Have you ever had to forgive someone? Was it very easy or very hard?

Forgiveness is part of life. Don't procrastinate. Forgive a misdeed as soon as possible and hope others will do the same for you. Forgiveness leads to acceptance. Acceptance leads to love. Love leads to happiness.

136

Do you feel like you are wasting precious time? When you are at work do you feel bored and feel there is no purpose to your job? How do you feel when you are sitting in traffic on your commute to work? Do you lie in bed too long in the morning? At night, do you watch too much TV before bedtime and don't get a good night's sleep? What are you doing about it?

Has a book ever made you laugh or giggle to yourself? Do you think the author was sharing happiness? How do you pass on your happiness to other people? When was the last time you made someone laugh?

Find ways to pass along your happiness to the strangers of the world. What a wonderful place this would be!

137

Are you living to work or working to live?

138

What do you really want?

You've got to make it grow on your own. Take time each day to plant the seeds (ideas). With a little water and nutrients, and a lot of determination, it will grow.

Start small, do what you desire with enthusiasm and stick with it. Growth will come and your life will be drastically changed forever. Write down five things you want to learn and grow. Next, figure out how you can include each one of them into your daily routine. If you don't have time for all five of them, then narrow it down to two or three you can manage. Or maybe decide the single most important thing you desire and attack it with passion.

Happiness is obtainable. Sometimes you have to approach your goals from a few different angles before you can find a way to grab it! Learning is a form of planting seeds. If you want something, then learn everything there is to know about it. Continue to do this over a long enough period of time and before you know it—you will have a tree!

139

Was there one time in your life when you made a mistake or did something that could have changed the rest of your life?

Your life can change in a split second. Accidents happen, bad judgments are made, wrong words are said. Think about people in prison who made the wrong decision in a split second. Be conscious and be aware of how you are living your life and treating others. Our lives can change drastically from day-to-day. Make sure you have filled your life with happiness and smile at the next person you see, no matter what they look like.

140

Does exercise make you happy?

Of course, we all know about endorphins, a chemical in your body that is produced during exercise. But there are many reasons exercise can make you happy. Here are just a few: you are managing your own health, you will look and feel better, you may be fighting disease, it is good for your brain, you will look better in clothes, the survival of the fittest! Now get out there and do something physical!

141

How often do you meditate?

If you have never tried meditation, it is a wonderful way to become more present and bring immense focus to your life. Don't be intimidated. Basically, meditation is doing and thinking nothing and focusing your energy within. There are a lot of great meditation workshops or retreats available. Sometimes it just takes being a little curious to find additional happiness in your life.

142

How do you commute to work? Do you find more happiness driving your car, taking the bus, riding your bike, or walking to work? Which form of transportation stresses you out the most? How can you change your daily commute to make it more joyful?

Walking or cycling to work is a great way to prepare for a long day of work. It also serves as an easy way to get your daily exercise without having to go to the gym. If you live close enough to walk or cycle to work, try leaving your car at home once or twice a week and use the machine we call a body. It is a great way to start the day off refreshed and in a positive frame of mind!

143

Are you good or bad at managing your time? Do you always feel like you don't have enough time in your day? If so, what can you remove from your day to give yourself more time?

Time is your most valuable asset. Itemize what activities make up your daily routine for a week or two. Once you have identified your routines, decide which ones you can live without or replace. Be conscious of your time and use it to your benefit. If you are always in a rush, remove something from your daily routine that does not bring you joy. You will quickly start to see which routines dominate your day. If you focus on which activities are most important, you can quickly eliminate activities that are time wasters. Slow down!!!

144

What does your upbeat music playlist look like? Does it put you in a good mood if you are having a bad day?

Music is a powerful source of happiness. The next time you are feeling down, put on some upbeat music, and let it take you on an adventure.

Follow excitement!

145

Who is the happiest person you know? Why do you think they are so happy? Can you learn from them?

Does happiness come from your work life, home life, or is it something we are born with?

It's amazing how some people are overflowing with happiness, while others look like death. Only you can make yourself happy, so stop waiting for others to make you happy.

146

When were you at the height of your skills? Maybe it was in a sport or in music. Do you still practice that activity?

No need to worry, everything is under control. You've still got it in you! Go out there and reinvent a past skill. In the past, you developed the skill because you enjoyed it and, most likely, you still enjoy it. So take the time in your life to rediscover your past happiness.

147

Would you be happier with one million dollars in your savings or a guaranteed salary of $50,000 for the rest of your life? How much money do you really need to be happy? Would you trade money for time? How many days of vacation do you get each year and is it enough?

Formulate a plan that allows you to work less and have more time off for yourself and your loved ones. Now is the time to have the life you have dreamed of having. There is no guarantee of tomorrow.

148

Are married people happier than single people? What age do you think people should get married? How does personal happiness relate to marriage? Why do you think there has been a shift in when people get married?

149

What is your ultimate happiness goal? Do you have a bucket list? How often do you check something off your bucket list?

Maintaining a bucket list is a great exercise because they are a reminder to experience new things. By experiencing new things, you are learning. Learning is one of the keys to living a fulfilling, happy life. Make changes to your bucket list as you grow and become aware.

150

Are you happier when you are thinner? Or, is your goal just to be fit and you don't give a crap about how fat or thin you are? Do you eat healthily?

Eating healthy is proven to make you happier in the long run. Make sure to be conscious of the things you are putting into your body. Your 65-year-old self will thank you!

151

What is the most meaningful gift you have ever given?

Here are some examples of meaningful gifts:
- » Anything you made yourself
- » A meal you cooked for a loved one
- » Time—an experience, a road trip, a journey shared
- » Something meaningful you wrapped in homemade paper
- » A story, song, or poem you wrote
- » A bouquet you picked on the side of the road
- » A photograph
- » A book
- » Art

Take some time to add to this list of meaningful gifts.

152

Have you ever thought about how you build personal relationships? Are most of your relationships with friends or family members totally random? Do you put a lot of effort into communicating with them? Do you let them know when you are thinking about them? Do you schedule "dates" or just wait for them to contact you? Do you include your favorite people in "nights out" and introduce them to other friends?

Contact three people today. Do it every day.

153

Do you consider yourself to be inclusive of others? Are you open and approachable?

In a group of people, invite others to share in the conversation. You don't want to always be the center of attention. Ask questions. Keep an open mind, an open heart, and a smile on your face. Others will notice and will do likewise. Sharing is a logical path to happiness.

154

Are you setting goals for a financially sound future? Are you saving money to accomplish those goals? Do you have a written plan for the future? Would you like to retire early? Spend more time with your family while you are still young? Do you know that all of these questions are choices that you can make?

155

On a minimalist scale of one to ten, where would you rank yourself? With one being a hoarder and ten being an extreme minimalist (basically living out of two suitcases). At what point does buying stuff stop being fulfilling and start to be a drag on your life? Would you trade ninety percent of your stuff in for its original value? How much money do you think you would receive?

156

Do you find more happiness from being right or being kind? Do you normally acknowledge your correctness to others? Or do you keep it to yourself? How does the other person feel when you announce: "I told you so!"?

There is more joy in being kind than in being right. You will actually learn more by calmly discussing the topic at hand and listening to what the other person has to say. Most things don't really matter in the long run, so don't take life so seriously.

157

Do you find happiness in travel and learning about foreign cultures?

Traveling is a great way to learn that people are all pretty much the same. Visiting old cities is like traveling back in time. If you are from the United States and you have never been to Europe—GO! Go to London. Go to Rome. Then, start traveling to the smaller, more unknown cities like Plovdiv, Bulgaria, and Maastricht, Netherlands. The smaller cities are where you will find the most original culture. The more you travel, the more you start to realize the true journey is within yourself. Go out and explore, your life will be better for it.

158

What is your motivation?

Focus your learning on a new passion every two years to stay motivated. A lot of people try to learn everything all at once and end up never accomplishing anything. Pick a project you are passionate about and devote two years of your life to it. The project might be writing a book, starting a business, or learning graphic design. Once those two years are up, start planning for the next chapter of your life with another project. Or, you may want to continue to develop your passion to become an expert!

159

Have you ever received a gift and at that moment it made you happy beyond belief?

Maybe it was a job, or a sibling or parent you knew nothing about was revealed to you. Perhaps a loved one who had been diagnosed with a deadly disease when a cure was found, or suddenly enough money to pay a bill you were afraid you couldn't pay. The concept of "pay it forward" is not new. When you receive such a gift, you may feel obligated to "pay it forward". Spread the joy. Someone somewhere is in need of a gift.

160

Are you happy when you are most productive? Why is there so much pressure to be great, to be rich? Do you think greatness or wealth make you happier? Why do people want to be recognized? Is it part of evolution? Why not be great on your own terms?

Find something you love to do and become a connoisseur. Be an expert in your field. If someone notices you—great! If not, the worst-case scenario is you had fun doing it. Be happy with yourself first and the rest will follow!

161

Do you have at least one person you can talk to? Someone you can completely trust not to spread rumors or pass judgment on what you have to say?

Man was never meant to be an island. Find that person in your life.

162

How much time do you spend outdoors? Do you avoid the weather?

Dress for the weather. You don't need to wear expensive gear. If it's cold, layer up! If it's rainy, put on your rubber boots and splash around in the puddles. Here are more suggestions what to do once you go outside:

» Make a habit of sitting on your porch, patio, or balcony and have a cup of joe or tea
» Lie down in a grassy field and feel the wind
» Go sledding
» Put on a pair of shades and pretend to be a movie star
» Create a secret garden
» Walk around the block and visit your neighbors

Find something to do outdoors every day, no matter the weather!

163

Are you a member of a religion? Do you practice yoga? Does prayer, meditation, reflection bring you peace? Do you practice spirituality alone or in a group? Do you have a private space where you can relieve stress or just be quiet?

Spirituality is the key to compassion. Compassion unlocks happiness in your life. Whatever level of spirituality you are comfortable with is your decision. Choose a path that leads to happiness.

164

Are you a member of a particular religion? Do you reject organized religion, and is it not part of your life? Do you honor the teachings of Jesus Christ, Buddha, Allah? Do you pray, worship, meditate, reflect? Do you practice yoga? Are you a spiritual being?

165

Do you feel like you have just settled into a boring old routine?

Remind yourself that happiness is in the journey, not at an end destination. Stop blaming others for your unhappiness. Stop feeling like you are stuck. Become a doer and stop being a complainer. You are the lead singer in your rock band, so start acting like it. Only you can make yourself happy—no one else! Choose happiness every chance you get.

166

Do you keep a weekly or monthly budget?

Keeping a budget is one of the most important things you can do to maintain control of your life. Understanding your income, tracking your expenses, and managing your debt may lead to your ability to take that special trip, or perhaps retire early! Go online or read articles and books that will help you get the things you want from life.

167

How many miles do you walk each day?

Walking is beneficial to your happiness in many ways: sensory, physically, mentally, and emotionally— endorphins are free, and your brain loves them! Walking is a weight-bearing exercise that builds your bone structure. By walking 30 mins/day, 5 days/week, you may prevent osteoporosis. If you walked 2 blocks or 2 miles today, double it tomorrow.

168

Do you have a personal relationship with water?

Water is life-giving. Whether from drinking, bathing, soothing, swimming, exercise, or cleansing. Make a point to visit hot springs or cool springs as often as possible, you can find them all over the world. Nature provides them and many times they are free. Swim in a cool river. Bathe under a waterfall. Explore the bottom of the ocean. Hold your face up to the rain and stick your tongue out. Jump into an icy sea. Wade into the surf. Take a long healing soak in your own bathtub, use salts, scented oils, and light candles. Whatever makes you happy!

169

Does working make you happy? Do you enjoy physical labor, maybe getting dirty or sweaty? Does cleaning house or working in the yard give you the feeling of accomplishment?

The human body is designed for work (video games don't count). Using your muscles to do work builds strength, improves your mental outlook, and gives satisfaction when the work is completed. Never be afraid of a little hard work.

170

When was the last time you burst into song? How did it make you feel?

Maybe you were singing along to the radio. Maybe you didn't know all the words. Maybe you were singing Christmas carols in a choir, or an old TV series theme song like "Gilligan's Island". Perhaps you may not have sounded as good as you thought you did. It's ok. Singing makes you happy. Never shy away from singing your heart out. Others will join you!

171

Are you a dreamer?

Turn those dreams into reality by developing a step-by-step planning process that works for you. Then just follow the plan!

172

Do you enjoy organizing your life? Do you find satisfaction in being organized? How much effort would it take to get organized and lead an organized life from this day forward?

Getting started:

» Gather up your important documents (birth certificates, W-2/W-4 forms, tax documents, receipts from major purchases, credit card payments, and debt, etc.). Store them in a secure and accessible place
» File your bank statements, includes routing numbers and account numbers
» Keep a monthly or weekly budget, itemizing your income and expenditures
» Understand and track your investments—if you're not making money, consider making a change
» Keep track of health insurance payments and understand deductibles and maximum benefits for each year
» Be certain your vehicles are insured, and licenses/registrations are kept up to date and that you know where to find them

Each of us lives a very complex life. It is best to stay ahead of the family business rather than fall behind. You will be much happier and less fearful of the world around you if you can get organized and stay that way.

173

Can you remember the last time you expressed gratitude in writing?

Writing to say thank you makes you happy. A simple thank you card for a gift; a poem to express your feelings; a letter to your parents or grandparents—living or dead, thanking them for their contributions to the person you have become; a written "thank you" for a service that was provided to you; thanking your boss for a successful year; always thank your teachers in writing. Be specific when you thank someone, let them know they made a positive impact on your life.

174

Who was the last person you told you loved them? Do you say it often enough? How do you think that person feels when you show them affection? How does it make you feel?

Telling someone you love them is free and can bring happiness to another's life. Compliments are free as well. It costs nothing and can mean everything. The best part is that all of those compliments will most likely be returned to you and will bring more happiness in your life. Don't be afraid to open your heart and let others in!

175

Does anybody have any questions?

Write down a few questions you would like to include in your own question book on happiness. Don't hold back! Next, use them as personal journal entries. Writing down your questions and answering them is a great way to reflect on life. You could argue that life is just one question after another. In life, you go around seeking answers to questions. Each answer builds on the next. The more answers you collect the more interesting life becomes. The best part is there's always another question to ask. No one knows everything—thank goodness!

176

Of your high school and college classmates, who got the best job after graduation? Where are they now? Isn't amazing how much everyone changes and grows after high school? What characteristics do you think make people successful in life? Do you possess any of these characteristics? How do these characteristics change over time?

177

How great was it to be a teenager and how horrible was it at the same time? There were definitely peaks and valleys to being a teenager. Are you happier now that you are older and your life is more stable? Do you think being happy during your teenage years leads to a happy life? What have you learned as an adult that you would like to share with your teenage self?

178

What was the last thing you created? Remember being a kid in art class and painting with your fingers? Was that fun and what could you do now to relive that feeling?

Creativity is all about desire. Desire is a strong feeling of want or wishing for something. Creativity is problem-solving. Don't be afraid to suck at drawing, painting, or playing the guitar, as long as you enjoy it. In reality, anything you are brave enough to try, you are probably going to suck in the beginning. When you have the desire, you become passionate.

179

Do you eat your leafy green veggies every day?

Make this a "must-do". This one important thing could protect your health and might save your life someday. Being healthy is essential to being happy.

180

List the five most important things you own. What would your life be like if you had to give up any of these things?

Live consciously by thinking about the important things in your life and why you feel the way you do about them. It will bring more happiness into your life.

181

What is your favorite song, movie, book, and painting? Have you incorporated them into your daily life somehow?

The artwork in your house subliminally changes your mood when you pass by it. Make sure you are surrounding yourself with artwork which changes your mood for the better.

182

When was the last time you went on a picnic?

Picnics are generally outdoors, but don't have to be. Picnics are an opportunity to spread all your favorite foods and maybe some wine on a big blanket and just be in the present. Here are some picnic ideas you may not have thought of: on the deck of a ship, or on a small boat; in your living room with the kids; in the back of a horse-drawn wagon, down a dusty country lane; in an apple orchard after apple-picking; and, of course—picnic on the beach.

183

What is your purpose in life? What do you think you would tell your younger self?

Finding a purpose is a lifelong quest that we fortunately never obtain. Don't feel like you have to have all of the answers. How boring would it be if we did have all the answers! But it is important to identify your life goals and work toward achieving them. We've only got one life to live, so make it a good one! If you don't know where to start, you may try to work backward. Picture yourself near the end of your life and think about the most valuable thing you would have liked to achieve.

184

Do you have a close relationship with your family? Is there anything you could do to improve those relationships? Is there someone in your family who is difficult for you to relate to, or understand? Would you be happier if you had the kind of family who sticks together and is always "there for you"?

185

How easy is it for you to go into debt for a new car? New house?

There may be some really good reasons to go into debt. For example—sickness, to help out someone who is dear to you, an unexpected setback. Be very wary of going into debt for more stuff. The happiness you receive from stuff is generally short-lived. Debt is generally not.

Think of debt in terms of how many hours of your life you will be committing to pay off the new stuff. If your time is more valuable than the stuff, you may want to reconsider going into debt. Who knows! If you can stay debt-free and save your money, you may be able to retire while you are still young! Prioritize!

186

Is money necessary for happiness?

List three times you had fun without money. Now, list three times you had fun with money. Compare and contrast the two lists. We all have a relationship with money, and the sooner you figure out what your relationship is, the happier you will be. Don't chase after riches if they don't bring you happiness.

187

Do you know anyone who you could describe as ageless? What qualities make them ageless? What would it take for you to acquire those qualities?

Some "ageless" qualities that immediately come to mind: energetic, active, open-minded, willing, fascinated, hopeful, generous, accepting, forward-thinking, happy, forgiving, positive, joyful…

You may already possess some or all of these qualities. You may be able to think of more "ageless" qualities. You may need to do some work to get there.

188

If you could do one thing to improve your health, what would it be? Do you make annual appointments for a complete physical? Do you exercise daily? Are you aware of your nutritional habits? Do you have your vitals checked with some frequency? Are you aware of your cholesterol? Blood pressure? Would you be interested in starting a new activity, such as kayaking, pickleball, indoor climbing?

189

Do you know someone who projects positive energy in almost any circumstance? Does that person make you feel safe like everything is going to be all right?

One way or another, everything IS going to be all right! There may be some tough times, you may have to take the long road to get there. But in the end…everything is going to be all right! Be that person with positive energy who makes people feel safe.

190

Are you a collector? Are you collecting happiness?

The more sources of happiness in your life, the less dependent you are on any one source of happiness. Collect happiness. Approach happiness like you would your stock portfolio. The more stocks you own, the more diverse your portfolio is and the less risky it becomes. Name five things that you could include in your happiness portfolio. If one of your stocks takes a dive, you still have more in your portfolio.

191

Are you lonely? Do you spend most nights home alone? Do you have trouble starting a conversation with someone you don't know? Do you conjure up bad thoughts about people because you don't know them? Do you imagine others are happier than you because they have lots of friends?

This is a very difficult way to live and usually doesn't lead to happiness. You may need to give yourself a good talking to. Even if it is very difficult for you, join a book club, or your local Toastmasters chapter. You are guaranteed to make conversation and your opinions are welcome.

192

Are you a dragon slayer? Do you procrastinate and let your problems build up and become unmanageable? Are you overwhelmed with what to do next?

Just to get started, pick your smallest problem and solve it. Good work! Now, pick the problem that is going to make the biggest difference in your life. Solve it. Next, pick the problem that is going to affect most people. Solve it. Not so hard…poof! You are now a dragon slayer!

193

Are you living and working toward what you believe in or are you just going through the motions?

Break down your day into one-hour blocks. Here's what the average American's day looks like: Sleep (8 hours), work-related activities (10 hours), TV time (4 hours), meals (2 hours). There is a problem with this picture. You have no time for yourself to enjoy the activities which make you happy. Don't give in to being average. Be a superstar, it requires the same amount of energy!

194

Can you recall an occurrence or an event that happened to you, but that you could not explain? Do you think you have the ability to manifest events in your life? For example, if you envision yourself making $100,000 a year in five years, can you make that possible?

If you picture it and are willing to work hard, you can make it happen. Maybe you have already made this magic happen. I can tell you…this magic does happen!

195

What is the happiest place in your life? It might be a coffee shop, a movie theatre, or a music venue? When was the last time you visited your happy place?

Identifying your happy place is easy. Finding the time to go there is the hard part. This is something you should schedule on your calendar. Share your happy place with someone you would like to get to know.

196

Do you allow yourself time to suffer through a loss? When was the last time you grieved?

Whether you have lost a job, a friend or loved one, a pet, or something you felt deeply for, allow time to grieve. Honor or memorialize your loss. Plant a tree, create a marker, write a story or poem. You may find the pain will be a little easier to manage. Take time to heal.

197

Do you think happiness contributes to a higher life expectancy?

Maybe the happier you are the longer you live. If this was the case, we would all be more conscious about increasing happiness in our life.

198

Does conserving, recycling, re-using make you happy? Do you have an idea what your carbon footprint is? Are you aware that biking and walking uses no fossil fuels and provides you with health benefits? Have you ever been to the dump to see how much utter waste Americans generate? Did you know that the US sells and ships our waste to China where it is disposed of? Did you know that Goodwill Industries and other thrift or resale shops ship used goods overseas to Africa and South America because they can't possibly re-distribute the articles brought in every day? Do you continue to buy new clothes even though you have a closet full of clothes you rarely wear? Are your kitchen cabinets full of dishes, cookware, the glassware you never use? How could you reduce the amount of waste you and your family produce starting today? What can you recycle today that would help you become more organized?

Maybe we could all get by with a little less stuff. Do your part to make the planet a little less wasteful.

199

List the five most important people in your life. How have they made your life happier?

200

Have you ever designed and decorated your own happy space? Do you have a seldom-used closet, a tree you can climb, a beautiful view out of a window in your home or living space, a spare bedroom that sits empty most of the time, a desktop or tabletop, or maybe a space beside your bed to claim for your own?

Here are a few ideas for happy spaces:

» A window seat for reading or writing
» A closet office or crafting space
» Build your own tree house/hideout (a kid can do it, why not you?)
» Turn your nightstand into a "me" space for journaling, reading, writing
» Create a space in your living room for prayer or meditation using cushions, prayer beads, your favorite art objects (if done correctly, no one will know, but you!)
» Assemble all your sewing notions in a basket beside your favorite chair
» A potting table in your backyard
» An office that converts into a dining room table

Most importantly, a space to call your own to grow your happiness portfolio!

201

What is your favorite movie series or genre? When is the last time you had a weekend-long binge, watching them and sharing the movies with friends and family?

Pick your favorite movie to share with friends, just like you would the Super Bowl. Buy a bunch of delicious food and invite your friends over and see what kind of happiness you can find. Maybe even throw a themed party where everyone dresses up as their favorite characters.

202

Does it make you happier to buy something on sale or to spend a little bit more and get something of better quality that might last a lifetime? For example, a jacket or a car.

Try to support companies that are trying to reduce waste by making strong, durable products. Maybe even buy from local companies to reduce shipping charges. In reality, we all wear our favorite clothes over and over. The rest just hangs in the closet for months and years.

203

Have you ever stayed at a stranger's house while traveling by using Couchsurfing, Warmshowers, or another social media site? What was the best experience you had?

The world is filled with amazing people willing to open up their house to you. Being a Couchsurfing host is a great way to meet fellow travelers and to live vicariously through them, even if you are working a nine-to-five job. Keep expanding your mind!

204

Do you find happiness in being very busy and having a lot of work to do? Are you happiest when you have a lot of free time? Do you find your quality of work is better when you are focused on one task or many?

Don't forget, we're all different. It is important you learn about your work cycles and the environment in which you thrive. When you're thriving, you're most likely happy.

205

Did you know: Your brain is programmed to operate most efficiently when you are being positive? So why not live a positive life?

It's true, we are happier and more productive when we are being positive. Negativity creates unwanted stress in your life and can lead to worry and disease. You will benefit from living a positive, healthy life, but so will family and friends and everyone else around you.

206

Do you have something you leave around the house to pick up and play with?

No, the TV remote control doesn't count. Bongos, yoga mats, harmonicas, guitars, cards, board games...all the fun things to leave around the house. Never stop being playful.

207

What books do you have lying around the house?

Books about art and artists may inspire you to create. Cookbooks or fitness books may lead you to spend more time cooking your own meals and becoming more healthy. Do it yourself books might make you want to build something. Books are a reflection of who we are. Don't ignore them. They are calling to you.

208

Have you ever thought about writing a book? Did you know that it is possible to write a 180-page book?

You can break down the task into the simplest terms. If you write two pages a day for three months (180 pages/90 days = 2 pages per day), you can share your thoughts, knowledge, and feelings. Sometimes achieving our goals just takes looking at them from a different angle.

209

Remember being a kid and running around in circles on the playground? Or playing kickball? Or having skipping races? Why do we stop those things as adults? What is the last game you played for fun?

210

When was the last time you made Valentines? Does it make you happy to think kind thoughts of those you love by creating a card or sending a note? Do you know someone who may need a Valentine, even though it's not Valentine's Day? Can you think of someone who may need to know that you love them?

Valentines originated during the persecution of the Christians. Those who were imprisoned received secret notes from their friends/relatives to give them hope and let them know they were loved. Homemade Valentines are fun to make. When you make a Valentine, you have that special person in mind. By making such a small gesture, you are double-dipping on happiness.

211

Skinny pants, collared shirt, tux, high heels, diamond earrings, fat wallet, fancy car. Which do you prefer? Does your appearance contribute to your happiness and who you are? What is your style?

212

Do you catch yourself judging others? Does it make you happy?

Judging others is a trap. When judging people, you are incorrectly assuming that you are better, smarter, prettier, more handsome, wealthier, etc. You make assumptions about how it is to walk in someone else's shoes, not knowing what it is like to be that person. It's likely you are judging someone who is less fortunate than you. Like you, most people are just trying to make it through the day. The next time you catch yourself judging, say to yourself, "I hope he/she is having a good day." or, "I hope they are happy." It is proven that judging leads to anxiety, whereas empathy leads to hope and love. Give others a break, and a smile. You might just make their day, and make you feel a lot better about yourself, too.

213

Can you think of someone who really needs you to send them a care package? What will you put in it?

Perhaps a child needs a care package of books or puzzles. Maybe your 90-year-old Great Aunt Angie could use a pretty scarf to boost her self esteem. Someone you know may need supplies but is going through a tough time financially. People need food…maybe you could send comfort foods to someone who is sick or help to feed a family in need. Quite frankly, almost anyone you know would love to receive a care package!

214

Where were you when you got your first kiss? Who was it with? Did you tell all of your friends or did you keep it a secret? Can you think of any other events in your life that you will never forget? Do you remember the emotions you felt during these events?

There are certain events in our lives we will never forget. Maybe the first time you drank alcohol or your first flight on an airplane. So much of our lives pass by before our eyes. We have a selective memory of the past. The future is unknown. Ensure you are fully aware of the present and live it with a smile!

215

Who do you look up to today? What do you admire about this person? What is there to learn from knowing them?

As we live our lives in stages, there is always someone we looked up to. As children, maybe it was our parents. In school, there may have been a favorite teacher. In college, we may have admired one of our professors. In the work environment, a mentor or boss. Maybe you can strive to be that person who someone is looking up to.

216

Do you have a BFF from grade school, high school, or college? Has it been a while since you reconnected? Do you know how to contact them?

BFF stands for "Best Friends FOREVER". If you haven't spoken to your BFF for years, you have broken a commitment. You shared your happy times and your deepest secrets with your BFF. Find them and reconnect!

217

Do you have a diversity of friends? Are some of your friends of another race? Do you have friends in a much different economic group than you? Do any of your friends have different interests? Speak another language? Live in another country?

Expand your horizons! Keep an open mind and an open heart to meeting new people. Life and happiness are about the people you meet and the friends you make. A diversity of friends can expose you to many new things. Ask questions, take the time to learn all about new friends. Learn to communicate in another language. Prove that diversity is a good thing. Make the world a better place, and you will receive happiness in return.

218

Are you a person of action? Do you tackle life with determination? Do you prefer to react to whatever life sends your way? Can you be assertive when the situation calls for it?

Be in charge of your life. Speak loudly with your actions.

219

Do you have regrets? Are there events in your life you would have done differently if given the chance? Are there people you would have treated differently? Would you be happier if you had a second chance?

Guess what! It may not be too late. Don't live with regret. Find a way to fix it! Sometimes giving a gift to the universe in honor of the person you feel you treated badly can ease the pain of regret.

220

If you could stop doing one thing that does not bring you happiness, what would it be? What would it take to eliminate that one thing from your life? What is keeping you from starting a process to eliminate that one thing and keep you on your logical journey to happiness? Maybe you could eliminate more than one thing that is detracting from your logical journey to happiness.

221

When was the last time you spoke to your next-door neighbor? Do you feel like you have a support group in your neighborhood or the town in which you live? Can your neighbors depend on you if they need your help? Can you depend on them?

Get to know your neighbors for a relationship that can be mutually beneficial. Invite them over for a glass of wine.

222

Do you consider yourself versatile or flexible? Are you rigid or stubborn, stuck in a rut?

Make three columns in your journal. Write "Versatile" at the top of the first column. Write "Rigid" at the top of the second column. For the third column, write "Happy". List the times you were Versatile or Rigid, and check whether it made you happy. You can determine for yourself what kind of person you want to be.

223

Do you have wanderlust, but feel powerless to live your dreams?

Always start small. Maybe spend Saturday at the open-air market on the other side of town. Or, pack a lunch in your backpack and ride 3 hours out of town on a country road. Pick the most scenic spot to eat your lunch (because this is what you do on a bike trip). Then ride 3 hours back home. Next, do a weekend in the next town from where you live. You can pitch a tent or go to a Bed and Breakfast. You may find it gets easier to make a change each time you take an adventure! Get creative! This is your journey to happiness.

224

Are you exercising your brain daily? Are you solving problems? Do you read every day? When was the last time you did a math problem? Do you practice your writing skills?

225

Have you evolved over time to become the person you want to be? Do you feel like you have been stagnant and stayed pretty much the same since high school? Do you know who that person you want to be is? What one thing can you do that could change the path of your life and make you happier today?

Happiness is the ultimate goal. If you are happy with the person you are today, be that person. If you feel a change is in order, solve the problem.

226

Do you practice loving acceptance in your life? What could you do in your daily interactions to welcome more love and understanding into your life?

Keep an open mind and an open heart. Welcome love and relationships into your life. Look for ways to bring more goodness into the world. You never have to look very far to find someone in need. Volunteer at your church, your kid's school. Do whatever brings happiness into your life. Chances are, you will make someone else happy in the process.

227

Have you ever been diagnosed with a deadly or debilitating disease? How did that make you feel? Do you think you have enough happiness in your portfolio to continue living as a happy person? What can you do to build your happiness portfolio in order to overcome such bad news? Do you have the support from your family and friends to discuss hard times when they occur?

228

Would it make you happy to turn your bathroom into a spa at very little cost?

Get all those candles out of the cabinet you stored them in. Schedule some "me time" on your calendar. Buy some bath salts and essential oils, and maybe a beauty mask at the grocery store. Hang up your bathrobe. Turn off the lights. Play some relaxing music and close your eyes. Don't come out until you're good and ready!

229

When you travel, do you research the historical significance of your destination?

By taking the time to explore your destination before you physically go there, you can open up a whole new world of learning. Here are some tips you may find interesting to explore: languages spoken, natural resources of the area, the ways residents make their living, best beaches, forests, mountain hikes, historical events, commerce, festivals, holidays celebrated, cuisine, weather, or anything else that might be of interest.

230

Have you ever found happiness in the mountains, a beach, or a river? Where were you and who were you with? What other things in your life make you feel alive? Have you felt this way in the past day, week, or month? When?

One of the most intense feelings is jumping into a cold mountain stream on a warm summer day; it makes you feel alive! Make it your intention to do more of the things that make you feel alive: the pain after a long run, a long dinner with friends, a hike through a foreign city, meeting someone new. Celebrate!!

231

What was your favorite board game as a kid? Have you played it lately? Why are board games so fun and exciting? Is it because of the actual game or who you are playing with? Have you ever tried to play a board game by yourself?

232

Who is the greatest horn player ever? Greatest guitarist? Greatest drummer? What do you do with the energy you get from music? If energy is neither created nor destroyed, where does it go? What do you do with your energy?

Music is energy.

233

Have you ever left a job or moved away from your life? How did it make you feel? Why don't we stop to acknowledge these feelings?

It's okay to turn inward and to explore those feelings. Be an individual and address yourself first. Happiness comes from within.

234

Are you happiest when you are alone or with a group of people? On a scale of one to ten, with one being completely alone and ten being with a large group of people, what number are you in the happiness scale?

Be conscious and realize that it is okay to be an individual! We all enjoy different things about life.

235

Do you think of people differently for how much or little money they have? Does it make you happy to think about a person's wealth? What about physical characteristics? Do you make judgments about a person according to what they wear? What they look like? How much they weigh?

236

What is the prettiest mountain range you've ever seen? The prettiest beach? The prettiest city? How did they make you feel? Have you been back? If you really love a place, have you considered moving to that place? Why not?

The world is filled with beautiful wonders. Make sure to include them in your life as often as possible.

237

As a kid, what cartoon made you the happiest? "What's up, Doc?" "Here I come to save the day!" "Go go gadget."

Cartoons played a big part in our childhood and the development of our creativity. Make sure to fuel your creativity as an adult. Find creative activities and entertainment to fill your days. We are happier when we are learning and creating.

238

If you could go anywhere in the world for a summer vacation, where would it be? Are you more of a city person or someone who likes their vacations to be an outdoor adventure? How can you save enough money to get there?

Maybe it is as easy as quitting your daily trip to the coffee shop or another unnecessary habit. Maybe you could save the change from every purchase in a big jar. Or, maybe your dream vacation doesn't cost as much as you thought it would. Maybe your vacation doesn't need to include five-star hotels and expensive dinners. Think about the vacation a little differently. Make your vacations about learning and experiencing the local people and their customs. Be brave and experience life differently than what you've imagined in the past!

239

When was the last time you visited a cemetery?

Don't forget where you came from. It is a powerful experience to walk through a cemetery, even if you don't have loved ones buried there. There are war heroes, grandparents, politicians, musicians, scientists, brothers and sisters, preachers, professors, doctors, etc… There is a whole community of interesting people there. Now picture them all looking at you from above and smiling at the wonders of the world. All of those people want you to be happy!

We are all part of the cycle of life. One day we will cease to exist. Make sure you are living your life on your own terms and accomplishing the things you set out to do. Be conscious of your life's purpose.

240

Do you have a favorite author or book?

Reading has been shown to improve your mental and physical health. Yet a quarter of Americans never read a book after graduation. Make it a point to find a favorite author and read all of their books. Reading is a great way to experience new thoughts and fictitious worlds. It's fun and educational. Learning is the key to happiness and reading is a fun way to learn. Keep exploring and learning for a happier and healthier life.

241

What is your favorite museum?

Museums are buildings of learning. Plan to visit a museum each time you travel to a new town or city. Many times, museums display artifacts that are peculiar to that part of the country or world. Art museums may have traveling exhibits from world-renowned artists. Maybe there is a museum in your own town that you have never visited.

242

Do you feel as if you can choose what lifestyle you want to live? Do you think you are stuck doing what you do because it is all you know? Are you bogged down in your job mainly for the purpose of paying off your debts? What change would you make that would give you more choices? Do you have a five-year plan? A ten-year plan? Do you want to be doing the same thing you are doing today?

243

Do you like to travel alone or with friends and family? What are some of the things you do when you are traveling alone you wouldn't do when traveling with others? Do you stay at nicer hotels when you travel alone or with someone else? Do you make a lot of travel plans and dinner reservations? Do you prefer to just wing it and see what happens? What do you hope to obtain from travel? Do you enjoy the rush from city to city or are you more into slow travel (walking/biking)?

244

Do you regret not spending more time with a family member or a loved one?

If that is the case, then right now reach out to the loved ones who are still in your life. We can't change the past and we don't know the future, so live for today.

245

Do you have anxiety? What causes your anxiety? Do you find it difficult to be around others because it makes you anxious?

One thing is for certain, anxiety does not lead to happiness. Find the answers to your questions about your anxiety through talk sessions, reading, journaling, praying, meditating. Get back on track in your journey to happiness. Anxiety is wasting your time.

246

What was the coolest t-shirt you have ever owned? Did you wear it until it was thin and soft? Do you still have it? What makes one article of clothing better than the others?

If you don't still have that favorite t-shirt, you should absolutely get a new one printed. We are creatures of habit. Maybe that t-shirt will bring back memories of a time when you were happy, impressionable, free, young, outspoken. Give it to yourself as a gift.

247

Do you think you could ride around the world on a bike or would you even want to? Where would you sleep? What life lessons would you learn? Do you think you would become a minimalist? What gives some people the passion and curiosity to accomplish such feats while many people are perfectly content to sit in front of a computer all day?

Alastair Humphreys rode around the world in four years. He did it on roughly $10,000!

248

What is your favorite Beatles song? Don't have a favorite song by the Beatles? Then what about the Rolling Stones or Led Zeppelin? What do the lyrics mean to you? Do you think we fill in the lyrics with the words we want to hear or what's on our minds?

Look up the lyrics of your favorite song. Most of the time the lyrics are really much different than they are in your head.

249

How can you help people who are less fortunate than yourself? Did you know that there are more than 60 million people in the world that are refugees?

Right there are 60 million possibilities to help someone.

250

Do you have a friend or friends who make you a better person? How often are you around them? What if you had five friends like that? Would you be a better person and happier?

Just another advantage of being an adult, we get to choose our friends. Make sure you are surrounding yourself by people who love the way you love others. If you have a friend who tends to be negative, find their value. Maybe you are coming into their lives when they need you the most. Perhaps they have been rejected. People thrive on acceptance, maybe you can give them some. If you don't have any friends, start looking in new places like yoga studios and dance classes. The world is filled with amazing people, make sure to take time to learn and grow with them!

251

Would you describe yourself as a happy person? Why or why not?

The best part of being happy usually means letting go and surrendering to the universe. Next time you have a negative thought, just picture that negative thought floating toward you like a big soap bubble, and when it hits you it pops and it's gone forever. Surrender to negativity, accept it for what it is and then let it go. We can't avoid all negativity, but we don't have to hold onto it. Be resilient and always sport a smile!

252

Are you happier with animals in your life? Which pet has brought the most happiness into your life? Have you thought about your friendship with your pet? When you speak to them, do they understand you? Do you understand when they are communicating with you? What is the source of this friendship? Is it the ability to help one another and to feel needed?

253

Do you ever watch old comedy shows on YouTube?

Type "Rodney Dangerfield" or "Andy Kaufman" and you will be entertained for hours. The best comedians master their stage presence. In your profession, humor can bring happiness to almost any day. For example, if you are a teacher, think about your classroom presence and delivery. Your students will enjoy learning and look forward to going to your class if you interject a little humor into each subject. Take your job seriously and be the best at what you do. But look for ways to incorporate a little timed humor into your day. You will have a more purposeful life and be more productive.

254

On a scale of one to ten, how happy are you? What changes can you make in your life to increase your happiness?

With ten being the happiest. Start focusing on finding happiness in your daily life and routines. If you gave yourself a low score, ask yourself why. If you gave yourself a six out of ten, then list four things you can do to get to ten on the happiness scale. Whatever points you are below ten, think of that many points or ways to improve your happiness. It requires more energy to be unhappy. Let's get started working on our happiness goals!

255

What is the biggest task or challenge in your life right now? How long do you think it will take to accomplish this huge task or goal?

Now, break down the challenge into daily, achievable tasks. Make it a point to make your daily goals so simple and easy to accomplish that all you have to do is show up. As you start to achieve the daily goals you begin to gain momentum and become more confident. Make sure that you are creating a reality that you can succeed in, not one you fail at on a daily basis.

256

Do you think if you work miserably hard today that it will lead to happiness in the future?

Don't sacrifice the present thinking you will be happier later on in life. Happiness is like anything you strive to achieve; you have to practice it all of the time. You decide what your journey to happiness is.

257

If you had it all, including happiness, what would your life look like? What songs would you include on your soundtrack?

Take twenty minutes to sit down and write one page on what your ideal life should look like. Be specific, ask for it all. Who knows, you might just get what you ask for! Take it a step further and cut out images from old magazines and make a collage of your ideal life. Exercise creativity at every opportunity!

258

When you watch TV or browse the internet, do you see celebrities who look happier than you? Why is that? Would you want to trade places with any of them? Who would it be? Have you noticed how celebrities all look beautiful? Do you think the key to being happy is being skinny and beautiful?

It's make believe, they are acting, so don't be fooled.

259

How many of these dance moves can you do: the twist, the monster mash, the flatulent llama, the popular girl, picking weeds, the dice roll, the robot, crazy legs, the octopus, two-step, opening the door, swing, the hustle, stir the pot? Having fun yet? Do you have any of your own original dance moves?

Next time you are out dancing, get your friends in a circle and go around the circle and each copy each other's move while chanting their name. Get funky with it!

260

Do you find more happiness in teaching or learning? When was the last time you were around a group of grade schoolers? They were all smiling, weren't they? Do you think it is easier to learn when you are happy and smiling? What about teaching? Are you a better teacher when you are smiling and enjoying yourself?

Pay attention next time you are in a learning environment and watch the people who are most engaged in the class to see if they are smiling or not!

261

What kind of friend are you? Are you the kind of friend you would like to have?

It is easy to judge others, but rarely do we hold ourselves accountable. Make sure you are treating others the way you want to be treated. Pass out compliments and be nice to others even when it is not expected. The positive energy you put out will come right back to you.

262

If math is everywhere, what formulas drive your life? For example, the amount of money you save each month, the number of miles you get out of each tank of gas, the number of hours you work per week?

Just maybe, it is worth your time to be conscious of the formulas in your life and to figure out how to use them to maximize your happiness. We all have a relationship with money, why not make it a good one!

263

What would it take for you to reduce your reliance on plastic?

Plastic is poisoning the earth we live in, and the animals we share it with. Be diligent in reducing the amount of plastic you use. Bring your own cloth bags to every store. Store foods in glass containers. Refuse plastic when it is offered to you. Buy products that are not packaged in plastic. Recycle whenever possible. Just say no to plastic!

264

When was the last time you hit a plateau? How did it make you feel? What did you do to get over the bump in the road? Do you have a plan for the next time you hit a plateau?

It happens to everyone. We go along being successful… until we are not. When you hit a plateau, move forward as quickly as possible. You may have to switch gears to keep the creative juices flowing. Paint something, write something, go to the gym for an endorphin boost. Don't spend a lot of time just hanging out on the plateau.

265

Does getting high make you happy? Is it a lasting high? Do you think people who do drink stimulants (coffee or tea) are overall happier than people who do not?

Name three other things in your life that give you a lasting high.

266

What color makes you happy? How can you use color in your life to make you and others happier?

The color red promotes energy and power. Orange provides warmth and joy. Yellow is the color of clarity and brightness. Green is associated with peace and rebirth. Blue brings balance and promotes sleep. Purple promotes creativity and problem-solving. Think about the spaces in which you work, sleep, and entertain, and use color appropriately. Surround yourself with the colors from which you will most benefit!

267

Why are some people not polite? Has social media enabled more and more people to be rude? What's with that? Do you really want to put your rudeness out to the world? Do you think people acted differently before social media? Does social media really make you happy?

Choose happiness…always!

268

Do you remember being a kid and sitting in the bathtub playing with toys? Can you still picture your childhood bathtub filled with toys? What did the bathroom look like? Where was the tub in the room? What toys did you play with? Did you prefer lots of bubbles and what flavor? Did you take a bath with your brothers/sisters?

Sometimes the simplest things in our lives can bring the most happiness and lasting memories. Tell me you weren't happy then! Now, when was the last time you sat in a bathtub and relaxed?

269

Have you ever thanked a veteran for their service?

It is the right thing to do.

270

What is the coolest car you have ever driven? How did it make you feel? Can you relate that feeling to anything else in your life? Maybe, getting a new house or putting in a swimming pool. What is the source of that happiness? There's no right or wrong answer, just be conscious of how physical possessions are brought into your life and for what reasons. Do you think paying for possessions with loans leads to happiness or are you better off paying in cash or downsizing?

271

Why do people follow the trends, whether fashion or other lifestyles? Are you so concerned with the opinions of others?

Think differently, adapt and live. Write down three ways you live your life differently than everyone else. Don't feel bad about being different because every single person on this planet is different!

272

Can you remember thinking to yourself: "This is a once in a lifetime!" What was the event? How old were you? Who were you with? Do you think may have more "once in a lifetime" events as you get older?

You should feel like every day is a "once in a lifetime" moment because it is. We only remember 10% of the past and we don't know the future, so make sure to live for the day! Carpe diem!

273

Think about a photo of yourself as a child. Can you remember that day and what happened before or after that photo? Were you happy or sad?

Life is a series of moments. Make each moment count. Be present.

274

What is the happiest memory you have of Easter? Did you hunt Easter eggs growing up? Do you hunt Easter eggs as an adult, maybe with children of your own?

The circle of life. If you want to make someone really happy, hide Easter eggs for your grandparents! You may know of another older person who might really enjoy putting eggs in their basket!

275

Why does doing the right thing make you happy?

Most people are fully aware of when they choose to do the wrong thing. We know that we are not going to feel good about it in the end. Be conscious. Treat others as you would have them treat you.

276

Do you find happiness in communicating? Can you think of one time that you were upset because you didn't communicate or couldn't communicate appropriately? How about one time when you did communicate and felt proud of yourself?

The better you are at communicating, the more successful you will be in life. Train yourself to be a communicator, and a fun and entertaining speaker!

277

What is the last thing you made with your hands (that wasn't on a computer)? Do you get satisfaction from creating something with your hands? Can you remember being a kid and getting excited about art class or wood shop? What were some of the creative projects you did in art class? As an adult, do you still utilize your creativity?

Don't forget that to be good at something, you must learn and do. In other words, don't be afraid to suck at something. We're better people for it!

278

What is your fondest memory of Independence Day? What summer activities usually accompany the holiday? What does independence mean to you? What other forms of independence do you have in your life?

Countries around the world celebrate their independence a little differently. Think of other forms of independence. Minimalism, financial independence, and moving out of your parent's house are all forms of independence. Be thankful about anything that makes you feel free.

279

What is the last story you told verbally? Who listens to your stories? Do you write your stories down?

The Iliad and Odyssey were verbal stories passed down for over 900 years before Homer wrote them down. Don't be afraid to tell stories and pass them down to your family and friends. It is a good way for you to connect with others and, who knows, maybe your stories will be passed on for 900 years as well!

280

Can you remember being in preschool or kindergarten and learning simple things like the alphabet, numbers, and colors? Were you happy learning those things? What are some of the cartoons or characters your kindergarten teacher used to teach the letters and colors? Did you use the Letter People or Sesame Street?

What is the equivalent to Sesame Street for adults? Why is it so difficult to find happiness in such simple things as an adult?

281

Do you remember getting your first suit or formal dress? Did it make you happy? What event did you wear it to? What purpose does a tie serve and who invented it? Did you know high heels weren't even invented for women? They were invented for Persian men a thousand years ago. The original high heels were used by men for horseback riding. So many things in life we take for granted. Don't ever stop asking questions and being curious.

282

What is the meaning of humanity? What is the purpose of your life? How does your purpose in life relate to the other eight billion people on this planet?

Life is a constant challenge. It is easy to feel overwhelmed and underappreciated. If you feel insignificant, stop right now. Don't let something miniscule stop you from living the gift you were given. Stop getting caught up in modern day worries and live your life to the fullest! Fill your life of things that make you happy. Get rid of things that don't bring joy into your life. Do something that benefits another human being.

283

What is the craziest thing you've ever done? Was it fun or scary at the time?

A few things that might come to mind: skydiving, running nude through a vineyard, cliff diving, crashing a wedding, sneaking backstage at a concert, running a marathon, throwing a dart at a world map and going there, sleeping under the stars, cycling across the country, going on a safari in Africa, the list goes on…you only have one life to live. Make sure to switch things up every once in a while, and try things outside of your normal routine or comfort zone. Most importantly, make time for happiness.

284

What are or were the best qualities of each of your grandparents? Can you picture their smiles? What was your favorite dish your grandmas used to make?

If your grandparents are still alive, give them a call and tell them you love them. Remember, you might be the last person who carries a memory of them. Make sure to tell your kids and grandkids about them. You have many of their characteristics, both good and not so good. Take time to write a page or two about each one. Make it permanent and leave it behind somewhere it will be found. Your memories will only fade, so make sure to do it sooner than later.

285

What would your perfect house look like? Big or small? In a city, small town, or the countryside? Would you spend your weekends differently if you had your dream house?

The practice of visualization is a powerful tool that can be practiced in many different ways. One way to use visualization is to spend time writing down your dreams in a morning journal. When you write your dreams down, it seems like they tend to come true more often than not. Don't be afraid to manifest!

286

What can you do to make someone around you happier? Are you acting as a mentor to a family member or a coworker?

It's not about what you have, it's what you can share. Take pride in who you are and recognize the things in your life that make you happy. When you are acting as a mentor to others you have an opportunity to be a positive influence. Make sure you are holding yourself with confidence and treating others with the same respect you would want from them. No matter who you are, you can share life experiences with others. Be a growth giver and help others. Everything you give to others will come right back to you.

287

What are your top five favorite books of all time? What do you think this says about you?

If you like the classics, then it might mean you long for the simple life. If you are more into science fiction, then you are drawn to the unknown and creativity. If you like historical fiction, you probably enjoy hearing friends and family members tell stories from the past. If you like non-fiction, you are learning new things all the time. Don't forget–books are knowledge–don't neglect your reading. If you are stuck and can't find a good book to read, ask a friend if you can borrow a few books.

288

How would you describe yourself in three words? How could you use these adjectives to bring more happiness into your life?

Here are some examples: curious, driven, thoughtful, nice, tall, crazy, outgoing, weird, talented, etc…

Write down some adjectives that immediately come to mind. Now that you have written them down, do a quick internet search with the adjective and happiness on the end of it. For example, weird happiness or outgoing happiness. See what the answer box (internet) has to suggest.

289

How do you think others would perceive you?

Be the best you can be, and others will get it!

290

What are the five best photographs you have ever taken? What is your photography style?

Once you have selected your five best photographs, print them and hang them around your house or office. Or maybe, make them into postcards to send to friends. Make sure you are leaving behind a memory of yourself and what better way to do it than a photograph or your artwork.

291

What is the most amazing thing you have ever witnessed? How did it make you feel? Is this feeling as strong today as it was at the moment?

Maybe it was a birth, a wedding, a concert, a sporting event, a monument, a sea, a ruin… The present moment is powerful, it makes us feel alive and it is filled with decisions. Next time you find yourself in a memorable moment, engage and enjoy it.

292

What did you do for fun in high school? What was the hardest you laughed with your best friend? In high school, was it common to spend a lot of time hanging out with your friends?

Every day of high school there was something going on, just hanging out at a friend's house or cruising in circles in your car. The teenage years are a strange time in life. Nothing is clear and life is like one big puzzle. It was difficult being a teenager but at the same time a huge adventure. Don't ever lose that feeling that your life is an adventure.

293

When was the last time you laughed so hard you cried? Why do we sometimes cry when we are happy? What other things in life make you cry from happiness?

Next time this happens, write it down and hide it in a place that you'll find it in a year or two. Maybe slip it in your favorite book or in the glove box of your car. It will bring you happiness when you least expect it. The world is filled with wonder and happiness. Be thankful to be alive!

294

Have you ever given a speech and totally rocked it? How did you prepare for it? What was your message? How many times have you struggled to communicate?

Public speaking is an art and a powerful skill. Self-expression can lead to happiness and understanding. Take time to develop your tools.

295

Can you think of a small thing that always makes you happy?

In Spain, all of the families go for a walk together at sunset. Every city has a promenade, Spaniards call them paseos, for their families to walk, enjoy nature together, and talk to one another. Spain has the second longest life expectancy in the world. Maybe activities like this have something to do with a longer, happier life.

296

If you had to be one age for the rest of your life, how old would you be? Why? As a teenager what skills or knowledge do you think you lacked? As an adult what physical abilities do you start to lose? Do you enjoy aging?

Each day that passes, you can become stronger and more comfortable with who you are. Don't lose your ability to adventure as an adult. Combine your experience with the curiosity of your youth and run with it. Life is precious. Don't feel like you are insufficient, because you are sufficient at plenty. Use your strengths to find happiness and become a better person. Do something in your life today to bring more excitement and happiness into it.

297

Why do kids not like doing schoolwork? When does the disconnect between learning and enjoyment happen? Do you think adults enjoy learning as much as kids?

If you are trying too hard at learning something and it stops being fun, take a step back and make it an event. It's not a race and it's not a competition. Learning is maximized when it is fun. Learning equals happiness!

298

Have you ever thought about taking a mini-adventure? Why is it that we feel the need to plan out every minute of our vacation? Don't we vacation for the adventure and to see new things?

Taking a mini-adventure is hopping on your bike or starting a hike for the weekend without hotel accommodations or plans. Try taking a day to wander around and follow the excitement. Talk to the locals, hop on a random bus, or take the train to the next town over. Live an adventure!

299

What is your favorite kind of sandwich?

Here are just a few: lobster roll, Reuben, egg salad, French dip, Sloppy Joe, hamburgers, hotdogs, BLT, Cuban, Banh-Mi Vietnamese Baguette, bocadillo, Philly cheesesteak, muffuletta, Italian sub, tuna melt, yummm there are so many. Makes me happy just thinking about it.

300

What time do you wake up for your job? Is it a struggle or do you just pop right out of bed?

Now think about when you were a kid on Christmas morning. The excitement of waking up! If you are not excited about going to work, something is wrong. Forty percent of your day consists of work and work-related activities. Make sure you love what you do or find a way to move on. Be conscious of how you are spending your time and how you are making happiness a part of it! To be happy, you have to love the life that you are living. You alone are responsible for your happiness. Start by visualizing what a happy life would look like. Write down the things that make you happy and post them in a place where you will routinely see them. Next, start making small daily adjustments toward that happy life. Nothing happens overnight, so be patient. Just like the seasons, changes take time.

301

Did movies like The Wizard of Oz and Willy Wonka bring happiness into your life? Or maybe it was Shrek? How many times did you watch some of the Disney movies? Why are adventure movies from childhood everlasting? Do you remember playing outside and re-enacting your favorite scenes?

As adults, adventures are less frequent. Life grinds to a halt as work takes over and monotonous routines fill the day. Be conscious of how you are spending your day and what routines you choose to fill your day with. Don't give in!

302

Should some people have to live in their cars to get a college degree? Is it fair that the average college graduate leaves school with $40,000 in debt and, on average, it takes them twenty years to pay off their student loans? Does this lead to happiness?

The system is broken, and it is putting more and more Americans at a disadvantage. The system is not producing happiness, it is only taking advantage of the youth of our nation. Any kind of debt is never a good place to start living as an adult. Find ways to avoid student debt.

303

Are you a sexual being?

High heels, top shirt button left undone, skinny jeans, a little flair for a night out…express yourself! Be creative. Maybe you can connect with someone.

304

Are you a creature of habit? Do you do the same things every Monday or Tuesday? Do steadfast routines make your life monotonous and BOOORING? What can you consciously do to welcome change in your life?

Try these recommendations:

> » Take a different way home from work
> » Once a week—use a new recipe
> » Change your exercise routine
> » Meet friends at a new restaurant
> » Call your long lost cousin
> » Go shopping in your closet and put together a new outfit

Just for the fun of it—think of ways to make your life more interesting!

305

What is the most relaxing thing you have ever done in your life? This month? This week? Today? How can you incorporate more relaxation into your life?

Time is the biggest variable. Make sure you are conscious of how you are using your time, don't waste it! Make sure you are incorporating happy, relaxing, and enjoyable activities into your routines. Make time to relax, even if you have to schedule it on your calendar!

306

What is the best Christmas present you ever opened? Do you remember feeling upset on Christmas morning because you didn't get what you wanted? Looking back on that disappointing moment, does it matter now? Can you even recall the gifts you gave last Christmas? If not, what can you change about your gifting strategy for next Christmas to bring a lasting memory of happiness into the minds of loved ones? Do you remember celebrating Christmas with your Grandma and Grandpa? What were their traditions? Do you find joy in passing down those traditions to the next generation?

307

Even though most of us earn a paycheck, when was the last time you earned money for something you created? A service you provided?

Earning a salary is important, especially when you have others depending on you. But there is a special pride in making something with your own two hands and discovering it is actually worth something. It could be something as simple as a paracord bracelet or a duct tape wallet. Doing chores to help someone may earn you some extra cash. Helping someone in need will make you happy, whether or not you get paid. Remember, happiness is all about adding value for self and others.

308

Do you like to be complimented? How frequently do you compliment others? Wouldn't the world be a better place if we focused on pointing out the goodness of people instead of judging or criticizing?

You can make someone very happy by commenting on their appearance. Most people put some thought what they wear each day or how they wear their hair. Almost everyone would like to be complimented.

People are especially proud of the work they do. Compliment someone on a job well-done, and notice the effect it has on them!

309

Can you think of someone you thought had everything, but let drugs ruined their life? Why would their happiness not be sustainable?

Be conscious of what you put into your body; your body is your temple of happiness. Life can change in the blink of an eye. It is important to constantly think about how you can improve your mental and physical health. Don't do drugs to impress others. Make sure you are doing things that enrich your life. Drugs can destroy lives.

310

Who is the smartest person you know? Does intelligence necessarily lead to success? What intangibles do you possess that could potentially leverage into more happiness?

As you get older you begin to realize your intelligence will only get you so far in life. There are other intangibles way more powerful than intelligence. The ability to persuade groups of people through speech is one intangible which comes to mind. Being a strong leader or working well in a group environment is another valuable intangible in life. Life isn't all about tangible monetary success, it's more often about the intangibles of happiness. Maybe you can start a list of intangible assets you possess. Here are a few more examples: organizational skills, persistence, problem solving, analytical abilities.

311

Are you the type of person who is generally early or late? Does it make you unhappy when someone is late or do you not care? How does it change your mood when a friend is late?

The little things in life can be disruptive. Make sure you are conscious of others and respect their time. Don't be the reason their happiness or mood gets derailed because you are running late. Happiness is waiting around every corner. Be aware of the simple habits that contribute to overall happiness.

312

What did you do during the summer as a kid? Did every day feel like an adventure? Who were your best friends during your childhood summers? Where are they now?

Being a kid is an exciting time in life because everything is new and a learning experience. Try to recapture this feeling as an adult. It's possible. The more time you can free up, the more time you have to explore and have adventures. Fight for your time. Don't give in to the daily monotonous routines that don't serve a purpose in life. If you're feeling stuck, do something you did as a kid that brought happiness into your life. Go for a bike ride, play a game out in the backyard, swing from a rope swing, do a cannonball off the diving board. That will get your fun spirit back in working order!

313

Can you recall the best meal or dining experience you have ever had? Who were you with? What made the meal memorable? Was it the food, the atmosphere, or the people who made the meal memorable? Can you come close to reproducing it? What is the best dish you can cook?

Food plays a major role in life. Not only do we need food to physically live, but food provides a way to socialize and make us merry. Make sure you are sharing your meals as often as possible with your loved ones. Meals don't have to be fancy or expensive to be good, a lot of times it is the people that make them enjoyable.

314

What are the smells that bring you back to your grandmother's kitchen? Fruits? Pies? Coffee? Thanksgiving? Dirty dishes? Chitlins and collard greens? Chicken broth? Laundry? As an adult, are you frequently brought back to your grandmother's kitchen from the smell in the air? Does it make you happy to think about your grandma and grandpa?

Life is short. Embrace the moments you have with loved ones.

315

Can you dance?

Hell yeah, you can! Don't let anyone tell you differently! If you enjoy dancing but you don't know how, take dance lessons. Dance classes are filled with both couples and single people. Don't think you can't take a dance lesson if you are single. If you really want a challenge, try taking Salsa lessons from a Spanish speaking teacher! Don't be afraid of sucking, because there are different levels of dance classes. The chances are you will even find someone that sucks worse than you! Wouldn't that be fun!

316

Do you consider yourself polite and respectful of others?

How you treat others is how you can expect to be treated. Say please and thank you, even for small considerations. Most people are just like you. They have many things going on in their lives. Someone might be having a really hard day, or a hard year, or a hard life. Everyone deserves your respect. Be mindful of others.

317

Have you ever had an epiphany? Did you act on the epiphany or just let it slip away?

An epiphany, by definition, is a sudden or striking realization. Maybe the epiphany was about a place you would love to go, or a person you would like to meet, a goal you want to accomplish. The time for positive change is now. Even if you only take the first step, then another, and another.

318

Do you have any memories of a time in your past when you were idyllically happy and peaceful? When you had time to daydream and reflect and things seemed to be going your way? Did you know there is an actual word for this?

The word is halcyon. We're constantly adding more and more things to our schedules, but rarely do we remove anything. We don't always have to be engaged. There can be a time of peace. It's okay to take time to do nothing. Take time to meditate, pray, or just sit on your patio and drink a glass of iced tea.

319

Have you ever tried Laughter Yoga?

Yes, Laughter Yoga is actually a type of yoga being practiced all around the world. It is a type of yoga which incorporates different types of laughter lessons and routines. People who have tried it, rave about how it releases stress and relaxes them. Don't be afraid to think differently and experiment with different ways to make you happy.

320

Are you free? Or, do you feel trapped in a situation that does not make you happy? Are you working toward setting yourself free?

Start small. Develop a step by step plan to freedom by listing what makes you feel trapped. Go through the list and write down what actions will set you free. You are in charge of your own happiness. You can make the choices that set you free. Freedom is essential to happiness.

321

What is your favorite story from your childhood? Who told or read you stories as a kid? Was it a big part of your childhood?

Once upon a time...those words excite! A good story takes you to another place or another time. Before the internet, before books, people told stories to document their history. Stories inform, inspire, and motivate. Make sure to pass along your own stories to anyone who'll listen. Being an entertaining storyteller is a great skill and it makes other people happy! Be creative!

322

Are you stressed out? Are you exhausted at the end of every day? Do you fall asleep worrying about falling behind in the schedule you create for yourself? Is your job making you sick?

You control your schedule. Design a schedule for yourself that is less stressful and more manageable. You may catch yourself telling others how busy you are. In reality, you are too busy because you make yourself too busy. Schedule yourself some "me time", even if it means putting it on your calendar. Work in some time so you don't rush to the next activity; stop and have a cup of coffee or tea, or do nothing. Stress can lead to poor health. Poor health does not lead to happiness.

323

Have you heard the old proverb: "What doesn't kill you, makes you stronger"? Can you think of a time in your life when this old saying proved to be true? What about a time you failed an exam or got fired from a job? How did you respond to your defeat? Did you come back stronger or did you shy away from the challenge?

Part of learning is failing and picking yourself up to try again. Alexander Graham Bell said, "I have not failed. I've just found 10,000 ways that won't work." The harder we work at something, the more purpose we bring into our lives and the better we become.

324

What was the best vacation you ever had as a kid? Did you have luxurious accommodations and gourmet food? Was it a rugged camping trip? Did it feel like an adventure or were you in the same resort the whole time? Do your memories include getting stuck in a thunderstorm or perfect weather?

As adults, we gravitate to all-inclusive resorts or cruise vacations, with all comforts provided, when our best memories come from times of hardship. Get out and explore! Find out how you perform under pressure. A camping trip to the closest national forest can present challenges and problem solving opportunities.

325

Do you consider yourself a happy person? What's your trick? How can you share your happiness with others in a humble way? Do you have co-workers who are habitually grumpy and rude? What makes their frame of mind different from yours?

Instead of letting the negativity of others get to you, make a point to overpower them with happiness and positivity. Part of being a happy person is sharing with others.

326

Have you ever thought of how to put your talents and passions to work? To earn money to support you and your family by doing something you love, or something you excel in? Have you ever considered a passive income to supplement your job until you can make your dreams come true? Are you thinking "out of the box" for changes in your lifestyle? Would you be brave enough to make a lifestyle change if you could? Would a lifestyle change make you happier?

327

Have you ever thought about traveling to Africa? Wouldn't you like to see giraffes, rhinos, cheetahs, and hippos? What is the most foreign place you have traveled to?

There are 54 countries in Africa, more than a quarter of the 195 countries in the world. Many of them are safer than the United States and have the most amazing wildlife. There are so many amazing places in the world to explore, don't limit yourself to the same capital cities most everyone else travels to.

328

As a kid, did you have a vegetable garden in your backyard? Was it fun to eat fresh veggies out of the garden? Did you get in trouble? Or maybe it made yourself sick from eating too many strawberries? Do you have a vegetable garden now? Does it make you happy to garden and grow plants?

329

Do you have an elder in your life who brings you happiness? What are some of the stories they have told you about their lifetime?

You probably bring just as much happiness into their lives. It's amazing to hear stories about Charles Lindbergh, who was the first person to make the first solo transatlantic flight in 1927. Stories from World War II are amazing! The world has changed so much in the last few generations. Don't lose sight of your beginnings. Keep in touch with your parents and grandparents. They are a treasure of the universe. We can all benefit from each other.

330

Do you ever feel like not talking? What do you do when you feel that way? What are three activities you enjoy doing by yourself?

We're all different and there is no right answer. It is perfectly all right to find happiness in a long walk, a book, or music. Not every second of every day has to involve another person. Expand your mind and try to think of other things you like to do by yourself. Maybe it's meditating, taking a spa day, or traveling alone. Think about it and try new things.

331

Is there one important thing in your life you feel is missing? What is it?

For example, a partner, kids, or more free time. A lot of the time we know what is missing but we talk ourselves out of pursuing it. Stop worrying. Start doing. Go get it!

332

Have you ever created a website or a blog? Did you give up after a month or two? Why did it fail or succeed? Did your blog or website reflect your passions in life? What are the first three websites you check every day? Why do you check them? Do they bring happiness to your life or are they just a way to waste time? Why waste time if it is your most valuable asset?

Creating a blog or website is a brilliant idea. If you have a passion you want to share with the world, be informed that blogs and websites require maintenance. Be aware, sometimes maintenance leads to burn out. A lot of people are afraid of failing or afraid of what others will think of them—don't play that game! Take a chance, if that is what you want to do!

333

What is something you do all of the time that you dislike, but you still do it anyway? Mowing the lawn? Cleaning the bathroom? Commuting to work? Paying the bills? How can you make a change in your life to streamline the things you dislike and do more of the things that make you happy?

334

Generally speaking, are you happy?

If your answer is yes, make sure you are sharing your happiness with people who need it. If your answer is no, right now is the time to make a change. Maybe try saying a happiness affirmation when things aren't going your way. It's as easy as saying, "I have everything I need to be happy right now!"

335

What is the value of your life? How do you measure it? Would you measure it by the number of kind deeds? By how many friends you have? By the amount of wealth you have accrued? By the places you have traveled or the books you have read? Or, by the hope you have inspired?

336

Have you ever done something that changed the world to make it a better place?

It can be as simple as helping a person through a tough time or writing a poem! Remember, you make the choice to save the world and make it a happier place. Set your goals, track your status.

337

What is the funniest thing your mom or dad has ever done? Were they trying to embarrass you when you were a kid? Isn't it fun to just think of such things?

338

Who do you think are happier: people who live in the country or people who live in a city? Who's healthier? How does living in the city or country contribute to your happiness? Who's more creative?

The point is, try out different lifestyles to see what makes you happy. You can make a change of pace in your life. Don't just settle for the lifestyle you were given because that is all you have ever known! It is within your power to make a change, if that is what you desire. Explore your passions.

339

Do you find happiness in physically connecting with someone? Why don't people hug each other more often? Why not share more physical affection with the ones you love?

Showing affection to a loved one is a double dose of happiness and creates higher self-esteem for both of you.

340

Where is the coolest place you have ever been? Why was it cool? Have you been back?

Life experiences are a great source of happiness. There is happiness in learning new things and pushing your limits.

341

What does your appearance say about you as a person? Do you find happiness in your personal appearance? Are you the best you can be?

Your personal appearance is a reflection of who you are. You can show confidence through your appearance. Untidiness might reflect an unorganized or lazy person. But don't forget, you can't always judge a book by its cover. A successful person may be hiding in ragged clothes. Think Pablo Picasso!

342

Does the reading or watching news make you happy or sad?

Instead of waiting for change to happen from the top down, make changes from the bottom up. If you are feeling unhappy with your life, make a change by making someone else happy. Whatever you give or share, eventually comes right back to you. Take responsibility for the positive change in your life.

343

What lesson would you want to pass on to others? What lessons or stories do you think your grandparents would have passed along?

You and your family have a history. Take time to write or tell stories to your family members. Document your life. You have experiences to share from which others can benefit.

344

When was the last time you stretched, did yoga, or meditated? Have you ever felt anything but happiness while doing those things? Is yoga or stretching part of your daily routine?

Yoga is a good way to check in on your body and see where you are carrying stress through aches and pains. If you're more conscious of where you are carrying stress, you can work on those places to relieve it.

345

Are you having fun yet?

Don't forget to celebrate. Here are some good excuses: celebrate your friendships, a day at work when you did NOT have to put out any fires, achievement of a long-term goal, finding your soulmate—at last, the end of a semester, the beginning of a new year, finding the best pizza place in town. I bet you can think of other reasons to celebrate!

346

What is your happiest memory of a pet? What is the saddest memory of a pet? Why are dog people...dog people...and...cat people...cat people?

Animals are a gift. They make sure we are not lonely, keep us fit, teach us responsibility, and show us how to love one another. If you are in a situation where you are able to own a pet, then do! Pets are a great source of love and happiness.

347

Do you start your day with happy songs?

Music can put a spin on your whole day (pun intended).
Create a morning playlist or two. Design the first play list
with lots of energy. Make another playlist that wakes you
up slowly, maybe more meditative at first. Experiment.
This could be the change you needed!

348

What is the happiest breath you've ever taken? Was it
at the top of a mountain or in the middle of an ice cold
river? Or maybe at the end of a long race? A sigh at the
end of a really hot kiss? The scent of a beautiful rose?

Be mindful of your breath.

349

Do you take things for granted? What about the freshness of vegetables that are in season? When was the last time you took a bite of a fresh vegetable or fruit from the garden? Or strawberries right out of the field? Were the flavors electric and made you feel alive?

Pay attention to the little things in life that bring you happiness.

350

What is your favorite dessert?

Ice cream, cheesecake, brownies, chocolate chip cookies, apple pie, carrot cake, tiramisu, red velvet cake, pumpkin pie, Rice Krispies treats! Food is pure happiness!

351

Is happiness contagious? Can you walk into a room with a smile and change the mood of the entire room? Smiling is proven to make us happier, why not do it more often?

352

Have you ever noticed how happy a cat is? A cat is easily amused by a shoelace or a string. Are you capable of being entertained by something as simple as a string or a stick? When is the last time you skipped a rock?

As kids, we could play with sticks and rocks, or a pile of dirt for hours. Give three examples of simple things that bring happiness to your adult life. It is important to continually find ways to bring more enjoyment into our lives. Spend less time with technology and more time with simple things from nature. Sometimes, it doesn't take much to find happiness.

353

How do you accept bad news? What is your first reaction? Do you immediately start problem solving? Do you try to put a positive spin on how to make it better? Do you instantly go to a bad place and stay there? Do you try to find a way to help others who may be affected? Surf the internet for possible solutions? Or do you go into avoidance mode and take a nap, hoping it will all be resolved when you wake up?

This question deserves your prompt thought and consideration. Life can be filled with bad news at times. This too shall pass, and happiness may be just around the corner.

354

Are you a list maker? Do you find notes to self all around your workspace? Grocery lists? Things to do lists? Christmas lists? Meals for the week? People you need to call?

List making is an excellent organizational tool. Use in moderation, as needed, but don't let it become an obsession.

355

If you were stranded on an island and could choose one personal possession to make you happy, what would it be?

I would choose a book.

356

What was your favorite pair of jeans or shirt of all time? Was it pure happiness every time you wore them? Now think of all of the clothes in your closet you have never worn. Do they make you happy? Why not own four or five really high-quality shirts that you take pride in wearing? Do you really need more stuff?

What are some life experiences on your bucket list? Would you rather own more clothes or check something off your bucket list?

There's no need to be an excessive consumer. Save your money for things that really bring you everlasting happiness. Life experiences are everlasting and are much more fulfilling than a closet full of clothes. Here are a few cool experiences to add to your bucket list: Carnival in New Orleans, hike the Camino de Santiago in Spain, cycle across Germany and Austria along the Danube River, hike the Inca Trail to Machu Picchu, and learn a second language. I bet you know of some adventures of your own.

357

Do you ever get lost, on purpose?

With GPS, getting lost isn't as easy as it once was. A lot of learning and fun happens when you're lost. Especially if you are in a new city, exploring neighborhoods you've never been to before. Get lost!

358

Are you at ease with yourself? Are you comfortable in your own skin?

Make a list of your positive assets. Then, make a list of the negatives—those things you wish to improve upon. You may find that it won't take much work at all to be happy with who you are.

359

When was the last time you had a moment of serendipity, when you felt like fate was on your side? Maybe meeting someone that made you feel like it was meant to be? The person you always dreamed of? Do you believe in magic?

360

What are your favorite, ugly comfy clothes? How often do you wear them? How do you feel when you have them on? Would it make you happy to dress like that all the time?

It must go back to a simpler time, childhood. Wearing PJ's to watch cartoons, putting on sweats to play outside. The uglier and more comfortable the clothes, the better! Do what makes you happy!

361

When was the last time you gave someone an award for a job well-done? Did it make you happy? Did it make them happy?

Once I got an award for being a "Good ol' sole". It was the sole of a found boot, spray-painted gold, with an embossed emblem stapled to a piece of scrap lumber. I will remember it always! Maybe the best award ever! Almost everyone deserves an award, especially if it brings a little humor and happiness into someone's life.

362

Do you belong to a tribe? Are you a member of a team? Are you the fan who wears a jersey or team logo on game day? Does it make you happy to have a sense of belonging?

Humans are a gregarious species. We need each other, depend on each other. Like it or not, we are all members of a tribe, sometimes based on religion, politics, proximity, family, language, work relationships. Tribal unity makes us happy.

363

Have you ever swam in an ocean? Do you remember the first time you saw an ocean or a sea? On the flipside. What would it be like to grow up on an island? What about the first time you saw snow?

It's hard to imagine, but some people have never seen things as common as snow and oceans. Don't be afraid to get away and to explore the rest of the world. You will be better for it. If you can't afford to travel, then why not take a mini-adventure to the closest national forest or lake. There are inexpensive ways to travel and see the world. Get creative! There have been people who have cycled around the world by simply walking out their front door and getting on their bike!

364

What are your favorite foods? Can you fix them yourself? Does it make you happy to fix your favorite foods? Do you have friends who also enjoy your favorite foods? When was the last time you invited friends over to share your favorite foods?

365

Imagine yourself on your deathbed, what makes you most proud of the things you have accomplished? Were you happy? Did you do your best to make others happy? Have you reached nirvana—the highest state that someone can attain, a state of enlightenment, meaning a person's individual desires and suffering go away?

TO END IS TO BEGIN

ABOUT THE AUTHOR

SHANE DILLON is in the constant pursuit of adventure. Over the years, he has ridden his trusty bicycle, Disco, across the United States and twelve countries in Europe. Yes, the name of his bike is Disco. He came up with the name Disco as a joke. Most people think of going to a bar or discoteca as fun, whereas Shane thinks cycling across a country is fun.

Shane has a degree in Finance from the University of Missouri and an MBA in Wine Business from Sonoma State University. Currently, Shane is loving life, fulfilling his dream of living abroad in Spain. During the week he writes and teaches. On weekends and summers he adventures throughout Europe.

OTHER BOOKS BY SHANE DILLON

The Franklin Fi
A Personal Finance Adventure for Next Generation Investors

A personal finance novel for young adults and beginning investors. *The Franklin Fi* is a must read for anyone who has ever wanted to learn how to invest in the stock market, but has been too intimidated to learn.

The Franklin Fi is a riotous novel about four high schoolers learning how to invest in the stock market. The friends learn the hard way as they get their first jobs and begin to save for their futures. *The Franklin Fi* is the first installment of a three part series which sets the stage for the friends as they venture onto Wall Street.

The basis of *The Franklin Fi* is to provide upstart youth with their first personal finance lesson. Shane Dillon's aim is to demystify personal finance and provide a crash course toward achieving financial freedom in the future.

Made in the USA
Columbia, SC
13 December 2020

27745208R00121